November 2013

IMMIGRATION DETENTION

Additional Actions Could Strengthen DHS Efforts to Address Sexual Abuse

IMMIGRATION DETENTION

Additional Actions Could Strengthen DHS Efforts to Address Sexual Abuse

GAO Highlights

Highlights of GAO-14-38, a report to congressional requesters

Why GAO Did This Study

In 2003 Congress passed the Prison Rape Elimination Act (PREA) to protect individuals against sexual abuse and assault in confinement settings, including persons potentially subject to removal from the United States housed in DHS's detention facilities. GAO was asked to review DHS efforts to address issues of sexual abuse and assault in immigration detention facilities. This report examines (1) what DHS data show about sexual abuse and assault in immigration detention facilities, and how these data are used for detention management; (2) the extent to which DHS has included provisions for addressing sexual abuse and assault in its detention standards; and (3) the extent to which DHS has assessed compliance with these provisions and the results.

GAO reviewed documentation for 215 sexual abuse and assault allegations reported to ICE headquarters from October 2009 through March 2013; analyzed detention standards and inspection reports; and visited 10 detention facilities selected based on detainee population, among other things. The visit results cannot be generalized, but provided insight.

What GAO Recommends

GAO recommends that DHS (1) develop additional controls to ensure all allegations are reported to headquarters, (2) coordinate OIG access to hotline connectivity data, (3) document and maintain reliable information on detention standards, and (4) develop a process for performing oversight of SAAPI provisions consistently across facilities. DHS concurred and reported actions to address the recommendations.

View GAO-14-38. For more information, contact Rebecca Gambler at (202) 512-8777 or gambler@gao.gov.

What GAO Found

The Department of Homeland Security's (DHS) U.S. Immigration and Customs Enforcement (ICE) sexual abuse and assault allegations data are not complete, a fact that could limit their usefulness for detention management. ICE's data system described 215 allegations of sexual abuse and assault in facilities that had over 1.2 million admissions from October 2010 through March 2013; however, ICE data did not include all reported allegations. For example, GAO was unable to locate an additional 28 allegations detainees reported to the 10 facilities GAO visited—or 40 percent of 70 total allegations at these 10 facilities—because ICE field office officials did not report them to ICE headquarters. ICE issued guidance on reporting sexual abuse and assault allegations, but has not developed controls to ensure that field office officials responsible for overseeing all facilities are reporting allegations to ICE headquarters. Detainees may also face barriers to reporting abuse, such as difficulty reaching the DHS Office of Inspector General (OIG) telephone hotline, one of various means for reporting abuse. For example, GAO's review of data maintained by ICE's phone services contractor for fiscal years 2010 through 2012 showed that approximately 14 percent of calls placed to the hotline from about 210 facilities did not go through because, for example, the call was not answered. OIG officials were not aware that the OIG could monitor hotline connectivity through these data. Developing additional controls to better ensure reporting of allegations and coordinating with the OIG to better ensure OIG access to hotline connectivity data in accordance with federal internal control standards could better position ICE to assess its sexual abuse and assault prevention and intervention (SAAPI) efforts.

DHS included various SAAPI provisions in three of four sets of detention standards it uses at detention facilities, but does not have reliable and consistent information to determine which provisions apply to which individual facilities. For example, GAO's review of a nonprobability sample of 20 facility contracts and agreements showed inconsistencies in ICE's data on which detention standards should be in place for almost half of the facilities. Documenting and maintaining reliable information about which detention standards apply to which facilities in accordance with federal internal control standards could better ensure that ICE officials, facility administrators, and other stakeholders have a reliable and consistent understanding of facility requirements and position ICE to plan for SAAPI program operations.

DHS focused its sexual abuse and assault oversight on 157 of approximately 250 facilities that housed about 90 percent of detainees and found most facilities compliant with SAAPI provisions from fiscal years 2010 through 2013. ICE used various oversight mechanisms, such as inspections, onsite supervision, and facility self-assessments, and identified SAAPI-related deficiencies. However, facility inspection reports did not consistently assess all SAAPI provisions expected by inspection protocols. For example, during 27 percent of inspections performed during this time period inspectors did not assess whether facilities met the provision to have sexual abuse statistics and reports readily available for review. Developing a process for ensuring consistency across and completeness in how SAAPI inspections are performed in accordance with federal internal control standards could help ensure that ICE management has complete information about SAAPI compliance across all detention facilities.

_____ United States Government Accountability Office

Contents

Tables

Figures

Abbreviations

DHS	Department of Homeland Security
DOJ	Department of Justice
DSM	detention service manager
ERO	Enforcement and Removal Operations
HIV	Human Immunodeficiency Virus
ICE	U.S. Immigration and Customs Enforcement
JICMS	Joint Integrity Case Management System
NDS	National Detention Standards
NPREC	National Prison Rape Elimination Commission
OAQ	Office of Acquisition Management
ODO	Office of Detention Oversight
ODPP	Office of Detention Policy and Planning
OIG	Office of Inspector General
OPR	Office of Professional Responsibility
PBNDS	Performance-Based National Detention Standards
PREA	Prison Rape Elimination Act
SAAPI	sexual abuse and assault prevention and intervention
SAFE	sexual assault forensic examiner
SANE	sexual assault nurse examiner
USAO	U.S. Attorney's Office
USMS	U.S. Marshals Service

GAO

U.S. GOVERNMENT ACCOUNTABILITY OFFICE

441 G St. N.W.
Washington, DC 20548

November 20, 2013

Congressional Requesters

Congress passed the Prison Rape Elimination Act of 2003 (PREA) to protect individuals against sexual abuse and assault in confinement settings, including persons confined in U.S. immigration detention facilities.[1] From fiscal years 2010 through 2012, the Department of Homeland Security (DHS) admitted persons potentially subject to removal from the United States for violations of immigration law into its approximately 250 immigration detention facilities, which had more than 1.2 million admissions. The National Prison Rape Elimination Commission, which PREA established to study the impacts of prison rape in the United States, reported that persons in immigration detention facilities are especially vulnerable to sexual abuse and its effects because of social, cultural, and language isolation; poor understanding of U.S. culture and the subculture of U.S. prisons; and the often traumatic experiences they have endured in their cultures of origin. Furthermore, the National Prison Rape Elimination Commission reported that immigration detainees may be especially vulnerable to sexual abuse and assault by staff because detainees are confined by the same agency that has the power to deport them, and fearing the possibility of retaliatory deportation, tend to be less likely than other prisoners to challenge the conditions of their confinement.[2]

---

[1] Pub. L. No. 108-79, 117 Stat. 972 (codified at 42 U.S.C. §§ 15601-15609). PREA requires the Bureau of Justice Statistics within the Department of Justice to collect and disseminate information on the incidence of prison rape. 42 U.S.C. § 15603. As part of its PREA-related responsibilities, the Bureau of Justice Statistics reported in May 2013 that during 2011 and 2012, an estimated 4 percent of state and federal prison inmates and 3.2 percent of jail inmates reported experiencing one or more incidents of sexual victimization within the past 12 months or since admission to the facility, if detention had been less than 12 months. The Bureau of Justice Statistics also collected allegations of sexual abuse reported by detainees in 5 immigration detention facilities that collectively housed about 13 percent of the immigration detention population during fiscal years 2011 and 2012 and found that the percentage of detainees reporting having experienced sexual abuse across the facilities ranged from 0.8 to 3.8 percent; however, these data for detainees are not generalizable to all ICE detention facilities. See Department of Justice, Office of Justice Programs, Bureau of Justice Statistics, *Sexual Victimization in Prisons and Jails Reported by Inmates, 2011-12,* NCJ 241399 (Washington, D.C.: May 2013).

[2] See National Prison Rape Elimination Commission, *National Prison Rape Elimination Commission Report,* June 2009.

DHS's U.S. Immigration and Customs Enforcement (ICE) is responsible for overseeing the nation's largest civil detention system. Within ICE, the Office of Acquisition Management (OAQ) negotiates contracts and agreements with facilities to house detainees that incorporate various immigration detention standards for conditions of confinement. The Office of Detention Policy and Planning (ODPP) is responsible for detention system design and evaluation, and the Enforcement and Removal Operations (ERO) oversees the confinement of ICE detainees across facilities in accordance with immigration detention standards. In addition, the Office of Professional Responsibility (OPR) tracks and investigates sexual abuse and assault allegations in immigration detention facilities.

You asked us to review DHS's efforts to address issues of sexual abuse and assault in immigration detention facilities. This report addresses the following questions: (1) What do DHS data show about sexual abuse and assault in immigration detention facilities, and how are these data used for detention management? (2) To what extent has DHS included provisions for addressing sexual abuse and assault in its immigration detention standards? (3) To what extent has DHS assessed facility administrator compliance with these provisions and what were the results of DHS's assessments?

To address these questions, we assessed DHS's efforts to address sexual abuse and assault in immigration detention facilities that house ICE detainees.[3] In particular, we visited a nonprobability sample of 10 detention facilities in California, Florida, Texas, and Washington. We selected these facilities based on a mix of factors, such as differences in geographical location, detainee population, facility type, detention standards governing the facility, length of time the facility may hold detainees, and recommendations made by DHS and organizations that

---

[3]DHS defines an immigration detention facility as a confinement facility operated by or affiliated with ICE that routinely holds persons for over 24 hours pending resolution or completion of immigration removal operations or processes. We did not include other types of facilities, such as holding facilities and prisons that temporarily house detainees waiting for ICE transfer to detention facilities. We also excluded the three federal prisons where ICE has detention bed space because two of these facilities house few detainees and the use of the third prison for detention was to be discontinued by the end of calendar year 2013, according to Bureau of Prisons and ICE officials. We also did not include facilities for juveniles that are regulated by the Department of Health and Human Services.

work with immigration detainees.[4] We collected and reviewed investigative files for all 70 sexual abuse and assault allegations occurring from fiscal years 2010 through 2012 maintained at the 10 facilities we visited and assessed their completeness against ICE requirements and *Standards for Internal Control in the Federal Government*.[5] We interviewed ERO field office officials, facility personnel, and detainees regarding sexual abuse and assault prevention and intervention (SAAPI) policies and procedures in place at the facilities we visited.[6] In advance of each visit, we interviewed representatives from at least one local immigrant advocacy organization about their views on SAAPI efforts at the facilities.[7] The information we obtained from our facility visits cannot be generalized to all facilities, guards, detainees, or advocacy organizations, but offers insight into the overall range of implementation of SAAPI policies across detention facilities.

To determine what DHS data show about sexual abuse and assault in detention facilities and how they are used for detention management, we reviewed closing reports summarizing the allegation and investigative steps and outcomes for all 215 sexual abuse and assault allegations reported to ICE from October 2009 through March 2013 and tracked in

---

[4]We did not use the number of sexual abuse allegations at a facility as part of our selection criteria because a higher number of allegations could represent either (1) an increased risk of abuse to detainees or (2) increased reporting at a facility.

[5]GAO, *Standards for Internal Control in the Federal Government*, GAO/AIMD-00-21.3.1 (Washington, D.C.: Nov. 1, 1999). Of these files, we selected investigative files for a nonprobability sample of 15 allegations for more in-depth analysis, to include allegations from each facility and allegations against staff members and allegations against detainees. The results of our more in-depth analysis are not generalizable to all investigative files, but provided helpful insights into investigative file completeness.

[6]In particular, we interviewed a nonprobability sample of 18 guards at 9 facilities, which we selected to include 1 male and 1 female at each facility. Guards at 1 facility elected not to speak with us at the recommendation of their union, which was concerned that information guards shared with us could be used by facility management to negatively assess guard performance. In addition, we interviewed a nonprobability sample of 53 detainees at 9 facilities. The 10th facility did not have any detainees in its custody during our visit. We selected detainees based on gender, age, country of origin, and number of days in ICE custody.

[7]We identified these local organizations through recommendations provided by two national advocacy organizations—the American Civil Liberties Union and the National Immigrant Justice Center. In instances where the national organizations suggested that we speak with more than one local organization, we invited representatives from all of the local organizations to meet with us.

OPR's Joint Integrity Case Management System (JICMS)—the primary system ICE uses to track sexual abuse and assault allegations.[8] We also met with agency officials from ICE offices and other DHS components responsible for collecting and using data on sexual abuse and assault in detention facilities including the DHS Office of Inspector General (OIG), which investigates misconduct involving DHS and contractor employees and operates a hotline through which detainees can report complaints regarding misconduct in detention facilities, including sexual abuse and assault, and the DHS Office for Civil Rights and Civil Liberties, which is responsible for identifying policy gaps that can contribute to sexual abuse. To assess the reliability of the JICMS data, we compared the allegations contained in JICMS, which according to ICE is to include all reported sexual abuse and assault allegations, with other information sources including allegations documented by the 10 facilities we visited. Further, we interviewed knowledgeable OPR officials about the completeness and reliability of JICMS data and controls in place for these data. We used this information to assess ICE controls for maintaining JICMS data against ICE requirements and *Standards for Internal Control in the Federal Government*.[9] We determined that the data within JICMS were sufficiently reliable for the purpose of presenting the type and outcome of sexual abuse and assault allegations, but we found limitations with the information about the number of reported sexual abuse allegations in JICMS, which we discuss later in this report. We also conducted limited testing of mechanisms available to detainees for reporting sexual abuse at each of the facilities we visited by placing calls to ICE hotlines from selected telephones within detainee housing, among other things, and assessed these mechanisms against ICE detention standards requirements and *Standards for Internal Control in the Federal Government*.[10] In addition, we collected and analyzed telephone connectivity data from ERO to determine the extent to which detainee calls placed to the OIG hotline from fiscal years 2010 through 2012 using

---

[8]We selected October 2009 because, according to ICE officials, data prior to fiscal year 2010 do not include sexual abuse and assault allegations against detainees. According to ICE OPR, it did not collect this information in JICMS prior to fiscal year 2010 because the office was focused on employee and contractor misconduct rather than detainee misconduct. We selected March 2013 because OPR had completed most investigations into allegations made through then at the time of our review.

[9]GAO/AIMD-00-21.3.1.

[10]GAO/AIMD-00-21.3.1.

ICE's telephone contractor or its pro bono telephone platform were successfully connected.[11] We assessed the reliability of these data by interviewing ERO officials and contractor personnel familiar with the processes used to collect, record, and analyze the data, and determined that the data were sufficiently reliable for the purposes of our report. Finally, we assessed the completeness of documentation in a nonprobability sample of 15 sexual abuse and assault allegation files maintained at the 10 facilities we visited against ICE requirements and *Standards for Internal Control in the Federal Government*.[12]

To determine the extent to which DHS detention standards include SAAPI provisions, we reviewed relevant ICE SAAPI standards and policies currently applicable to, or proposed for, ICE detention facilities. In particular, to establish the relative protections these standards afford detainees, we analyzed and compared ICE's four sets of detention standards and DHS's December 2012 notice of proposed rulemaking for implementing PREA—*Standards to Prevent, Detect, and Respond to Sexual Abuse and Assault in Confinement Facilities*. In addition, we compared DHS's most recent set of detention standards—the 2011 Performance-Based National Detention Standards (PBNDS)—and notice of proposed rulemaking with National Prison Rape Elimination Commission recommendations for immigration detention facilities and also compared DHS's notice of proposed rulemaking and the Department of Justice's (DOJ) PREA rule. To determine which sexual abuse and assault standards ICE requires facilities to implement, we collected fiscal year 2013 detention standards data from ERO and OAQ and compared the maintenance of this data against *Standards for Internal Control in the Federal Government*.[13] We assessed the reliability of the ERO and OAQ detention standards data by reviewing the contracts on which the data were based for a nonprobability sample of 20 facilities, and interviewing

---

[11]ERO officials explained that ICE contracts with one telephone company to provide full telephone service for detainees at 18 of its 251 detention facilities. In addition, 191 facilities use this telephone company's nationwide pro bono platform, which enables detainees to place calls at no charge to certain numbers, including the OIG hotline.

[12]GAO/AIMD-00-21.3.1.

[13]GAO/AIMD-00-21.3.1.

ERO and OAQ officials about any discrepancies in the data.[14] We determined that the data were sufficiently reliable for the purpose of presenting trends in the standards to which different types of facilities are to adhere, but we found limitations with the data on the number of facilities that are obligated by their contracts or agreement with ICE to adhere to particular sets of detention standards, which we discuss later in the report.

To determine the extent to which DHS has assessed facility compliance with SAAPI provisions, as well as the results of these assessments, we analyzed and compared various oversight mechanisms, such as inspections, utilized at ICE's detention facilities. Specifically, we interviewed ICE officials responsible for facility oversight; ERO officials responsible for reviewing results from facility self-assessments; representatives from the ERO contractor responsible for conducting facility inspections; and DOJ officials responsible for assessing compliance with DOJ standards at facilities with which DOJ has agreements that house ICE detainees. We also reviewed the results of the 110 ERO and 30 Office of Detention Oversight (ODO) facility inspection reports that assessed compliance with SAAPI standards during fiscal years 2010 through 2013 to assess the extent to which inspectors found deficiencies in the SAAPI standards, associated corrective actions, and any patterns across reports.[15] We assessed the consistency with which the SAAPI inspections were performed in accordance with *Standards for Internal Control in the Federal Government*.[16] Additional details on our scope and methodology are contained in appendix I.

We conducted this performance audit from October 2012 through November 2013 in accordance with generally accepted government auditing standards. Those standards require that we plan and perform the

---

[14]We selected this sample to include (1) facilities at which we conducted site visits and (2) facilities for which ERO and OAQ information on facility standards differed. While not generalizable, this sample provided us with helpful insights into the reliability of ERO and OAQ's information on facility standards.

[15]We chose this time frame because prior to fiscal year 2010, the scope of ICE's inspections of the SAAPI standard was limited to 2 of its 251 facilities. In addition, our analysis included inspection reports available as of August 2013. At that time, all but 2 ERO and 3 Office of Detention Oversight inspections reports scheduled for fiscal year 2013 were available for our review.

[16]GAO/AIMD-00-21.3.1.

audit to obtain sufficient, appropriate evidence to provide a reasonable basis for our findings and conclusions based on our audit objectives. We believe that the evidence obtained provides a reasonable basis for our findings and conclusions based on our audit objectives.

Background

Legislation and Regulations Pertaining to Sexual Abuse and Assault in Confinement

PREA was enacted to, among other things, establish a zero-tolerance standard for rape in U.S. prisons and make the prevention of prison rape a top priority in each prison system.[17] PREA also charged the National Prison Rape Elimination Commission with recommending standards for addressing prison rape for consideration by the Attorney General and directed the Attorney General to adopt national standards for the detection, prevention, reduction, and punishment of prison rape.[18] In June 2009, the National Prison Rape Elimination Commission issued a report with recommended standards, including specific recommendations for facilities that house immigration detainees, and in May 2012, DOJ released a final rule for publication in the *Federal Register* adopting national standards for the detection and prevention of, and response to, prison rape.[19] When DOJ published its final rule, DOJ also announced its conclusion that PREA encompasses all federal confinement facilities, and noted that other federal departments with confinement facilities (including but not limited to DHS) would work with the Attorney General to issue rules or procedures that would satisfy the requirements of PREA.[20] In May 2012, the President also issued a memorandum directing all agencies with federal confinement facilities not already subject to DOJ's final rule to work with the Attorney General to propose, within 120 days of May 17, 2012, any rule or procedure necessary to satisfy the requirements of PREA and to finalize any such rules or procedures within

---

[17]42 U.S.C. § 15602(1)-(2).

[18]42 U.S.C. §§ 15606(e)(1), 15607(a).

[19]See National Prison Rape Elimination Commission, *National Prison Rape Elimination Commission Report*, June, 2009, and National Standards to Prevent, Detect, and Respond to Prison Rape, 77 Fed. Reg. 37,106 (June 20, 2012) (to be codified at 28 C.F.R. pt. 115).

[20]77 Fed. Reg. at 37,112-13.

240 days of their proposals.[21] On December 6, 2012, DHS released a notice of proposed rulemaking for publication in the *Federal Register* for adopting its own national standards for the detection and prevention of, and response to, sexual abuse and assault in confinement facilities.[22] According to DHS officials, the department did not have a planned date for releasing its final PREA rule, but anticipated doing so in fall 2013.[23]

Detainee Population and Detention Facility Structure

The Immigration and Nationality Act provides ICE with broad authority to detain aliens believed to be removable while awaiting a determination of whether they should be removed from the United States and mandates that ICE detain certain categories of aliens.[24] Aliens subject to mandatory detention include those arriving in the United States without documentation or with fraudulent documentation, those who are inadmissible or deportable on criminal or national security grounds, those certified as terrorist suspects, and those who have final orders of removal. Unlike criminal incarceration, immigration detention is not to be punitive; rather, ICE is to confine detainees for the administrative purpose of holding, processing, and preparing them for removal. According to ICE data, during 2012, the agency detained about 32,000 detainees in its detention facilities each day and held detainees for an average of about 28 days.[25] ICE detainees include a mix of men and women from a wide variety of countries and with criminal and noncriminal backgrounds.[26] For example, ICE's fiscal year 2012 detainee population was about 91

---

[21]White House, *Presidential Memorandum—Implementing the Prison Rape Elimination Act* (Washington, D.C.: May 2012).

[22]Standards to Prevent, Detect, and Respond to Sexual Abuse and Assault in Confinement Facilities, 77 Fed. Reg. 75,300 (Dec. 19, 2012).

[23]DHS officials also stated that the department provided its final PREA rule to the Office of Management and Budget for review in September 2013.

[24]8 U.S.C. §§ 1225, 1226, 1226a, 1231.

[25]These data are approximations for ICE detention facilities and do not include other types of facilities, such as holding facilities.

[26]ICE generally does not detain children, with the exception of children that the agency detains with their families at one family residential facility. ICE must transfer unaccompanied alien children less than 18 years of age who are unlawfully in the United States without a parent or other legal guardian to the Department of Health and Human Services Office of Refugee Resettlement's custody within 72 hours of determining that they are unaccompanied. *See* 8 U.S.C. § 1232(b)(3).

percent male and 9 percent female and came from almost 200 countries. When detention facilities admit aliens, they are to use a classification system through which they separate detainees by threat risk and special vulnerabilities by assigning them a custody level of low, medium, or high. From fiscal years 2010 through 2012, about 39 percent of ICE detainees were of a low custody level, 41 percent were of a medium custody level, and 20 percent were of a high custody level.[27]

ICE's ERO oversees the confinement of ICE detainees in approximately 250 detention facilities that it manages in conjunction with private contractors or under agreements with state and local governments.[28] Over 90 percent of facilities are operated under agreements with state and local governments and house about half of ICE detainees together with or separately from other confined populations. The remaining facilities house exclusively ICE detainees and are operated by a mixture of private contractors and ICE, state, and local government employees. Table 1 presents information about the number and types of facilities that ICE uses to house detainees, the entities that own and operate them, and the percentage of the detainee population confined in each facility type.

---

[27]ICE's custody classification system considers various factors including the detainee's most recent charge or conviction, the most serious conviction in the individual's criminal history, any other prior felony convictions, any attempts to escape from custody, if the individual has a history of assaultive behavior, and the individual's behavioral history.

[28]In addition to detention facilities, ICE also has 127 holding facilities, which are used by ICE, U.S Customs and Border Protection, and other DHS component agencies for temporary administrative detention of individuals for less than 24 hours pending transfer to a court, jail, prison, other agency, or other unit of the facility or agency.

Table 1: U.S. Immigration and Customs Enforcement (ICE) Detention Facility Types and Characteristics

Facility type	Description	Number of facilities[a]	Detainee population[b]
Service processing center	Facilities owned by ICE, operated by a mix of ICE employees and contractor staff, that exclusively house ICE detainees.	6	12%
Contract detention facility	Facilities owned and operated by private companies under direct ICE contracts that exclusively house ICE detainees.	7	19%
Dedicated intergovernmental service agreement	Facilities owned by state and local governments or private entities, operated under agreements with state and local governments, that exclusively house ICE detainees.	9[c]	22%
Family residential	Facility owned and operated by a local government entity that houses children and their families and exclusively houses ICE detainees.	1	<1%
Nondedicated intergovernmental service agreement	Facilities owned by state and local governments or private entities, operated under agreement by state and local governments, that house ICE detainees in addition to other confined populations (e.g., inmates), either together or separately.	103	34%
U.S. Marshals Service (USMS) intergovernmental agreement or contract	Facilities owned and operated by state and local governments or private entities under agreement or contract with USMS within the Department of Justice to house federal prisoners until they are acquitted or convicted. ICE takes out task orders against the USMS intergovernmental agreements and contracts to house immigration detainees at these facilities, either together with or separately from other populations.	125	14%

Source: GAO analysis of ICE information.

Notes: ICE authorizes facilities to house detainees for up to 72 hours or more than 72 hours. Of ICE's 251 facilities, 85 are authorized to house detainees for up to 72 hours. These consist of 31 nondedicated intergovernmental service agreement facilities and 54 USMS intergovernmental agreement facilities. In addition to the facilities listed in this table, ICE also uses 3 facilities operated by the DOJ Federal Bureau of Prisons to confine detainees.

[a]The number of each facility's type presented in this table is as of August 2013.

[b]Detainee population percentages are based on the average daily detainee population at facilities across fiscal years 2010 through 2012. Percentages do not sum to 100 because of rounding.

[c]ICE initially used 1 of these facilities as a family residential facility, but in 2009 converted it to a women-only facility.

ICE's detention facilities are located across the United States. In general, facilities that house the most detainees and exclusively ICE detainees are concentrated in the southern United States, while facilities that house fewer detainees are more evenly distributed across the nation. Figure 1 presents the locations of ICE's facilities by size and type.

Figure 1: U.S. Immigration and Customs Enforcement (ICE) Detention Facility Locations, as of August 2013

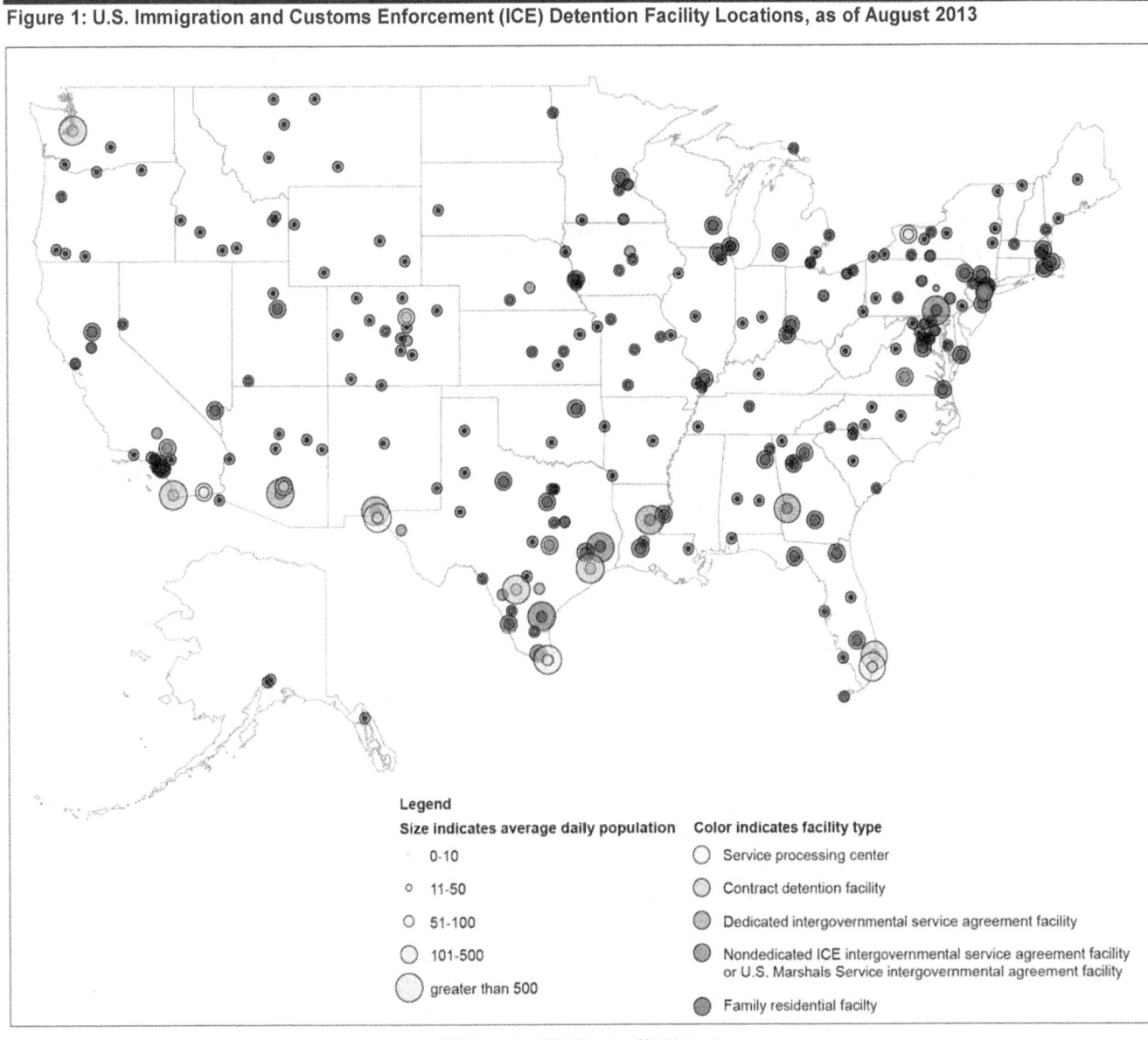

Legend

Size indicates average daily population
- 0-10
- 11-50
- 51-100
- 101-500
- greater than 500

Color indicates facility type
- Service processing center
- Contract detention facility
- Dedicated intergovernmental service agreement facility
- Nondedicated ICE intergovernmental service agreement facility or U.S. Marshals Service intergovernmental agreement facility
- Family residential facilty

Source: GAO analysis of ICE information; Mapinfo (map).

Note: Average daily population is based on ICE data for fiscal years 2010 through 2012.

Detention Standards

ICE uses four sets of national detention standards with varying requirements to govern the conditions of confinement in its detention facilities. ICE establishes the set of standards applicable to each detention facility through an individual contract or agreement with the facility. Accordingly, different facilities are governed by different standards. Table 2 provides information about each of these four sets of standards.

Table 2: U.S. Immigration and Customs Enforcement (ICE) Detention Standards

2000 National Detention Standards (NDS)	These standards are derived from the American Correctional Association's *Standards for Adult Local Detention Facilities*, Third Edition, and were developed by the former Immigration and Naturalization Service within the Department of Justice (DOJ) in consultation with various stakeholders, including the American Bar Association—an association of attorneys—and organizations involved in pro bono representation and advocacy for immigration detainees. Following the creation of the Department of Homeland Security (DHS) in 2002, DHS became responsible for immigration detention and began operating the detention system under the 2000 NDS.
2007 Family Residential Standards	ICE approved the Family Residential Standards in 2007 to apply to its facilities that house families in detention. The Family Residential Standards are based on ICE analysis of family detention operations and state statutes that affect children.
2008 Performance-Based National Detention Standards (PBNDS)	ICE revised the 2000 NDS to integrate changes included in, and move to a performance-based format more in line with, the American Correctional Association's *Performance-Based Standards for Adult Local Detention Facilities*, Fourth Edition. The 2008 PBNDS, which ICE developed in coordination with agency stakeholders to apply to adult detention populations, prescribe the expected outcomes of each detention standard and the expected practices required to achieve them. The 2008 PBNDS also include more detailed requirements for service processing centers and contract detention facilities.
2011 PBNDS	ICE revised the 2008 PBNDS to improve conditions of confinement in various ways, including medical and mental health services, access to legal services and religious opportunities, communication with detainees with no or limited English proficiency, the process for reporting and responding to complaints, and recreation and visitation. The 2011 PBNDS also expanded the more detailed requirements for service processing centers and contract detention facilities included in the 2008 PBNDS to dedicated intergovernmental service agreement facilities or, in some cases, to all facilities.

Source: GAO analysis of ICE information.

Note: U.S. Marshals Service intergovernmental agreement facilities are under agreements to adhere to DOJ detention standards. Facilities under private contract with the U.S. Marshals Service are to adhere to the Federal Performance-Based Detention Standards, which incorporate elements of American Correctional Association standards, DOJ standards, and the 2000 NDS.

DHS Agencies' Roles and Responsibilities

Within DHS, ICE has the primary responsibility for SAAPI in immigration detention facilities, but other components—including the OIG and Office for Civil Rights and Civil Liberties—also play a role by investigating sexual abuse allegations. Table 3 identifies the primary DHS components involved in SAAPI in detention facilities and their respective roles and responsibilities.

Table 3: Department of Homeland Security (DHS) Sexual Abuse and Assault Prevention and Intervention (SAAPI) Roles and Responsibilities in Detention Facilities

DHS components and offices	Roles and responsibilities pertaining to SAAPI
U.S. Immigration and Customs Enforcement (ICE)[a]	
Enforcement and Removal Operations (ERO)	• Identifies and apprehends removable aliens, detaining these individuals when it deems necessary, and removing them from the United States
Custody Management	• Contracts with inspectors to conduct routine inspections of certain detention facilities to assess compliance with ICE detention standards, including SAAPI standards, and develops corrective action plans, as necessary • Oversees the on-site Detention Monitoring Program, created in 2010, which places ICE detention service managers (DSM) at select facilities to monitor that conditions of confinement are in accordance with ICE detention standards, including SAAPI standards • Administers the ICE Community and Detainee Helpline, which detainees may use to report sexual abuse and assault, among other grievances
Field Operations	• Ensures that the appropriate components have been notified following an alleged sexual abuse or assault, and documents these notifications • Ensures that facilities are aware of response, intervention, and investigation mandates established by relevant detention standards following alleged sexual abuse or assault through personnel located at 24 field offices • Reviews annual self-assessments conducted by select facilities
Office of Detention Policy and Planning (ODPP)	• Leads efforts to design detention standards, including SAAPI standards, and was charged with designing a new civil detention system
Office of Professional Responsbility (OPR)	• Investigates select allegations of sexual abuse and assault • Documents allegations of sexual abuse and assault in the Joint Integrity Case Management System, a system to log, track, and manage cases for all OPR functions including investigations • Coordinates sexual abuse and assault investigations with federal, state, or local law enforcement or facility incident review personnel • Houses an agency-wide Prevention of Sexual Assault coordinator to develop, implement, and oversee ICEs SAAPI efforts
Office of Detention Oversight (ODO)	• Inspects facility compliance with detention standards, including SAAPI standards, using a risk-based methodology
Joint Intake Center	• Receives, processes, and assigns for review or investigation all misconduct allegations involving ICE and U.S. Customs and Border Protection employees and contractors, including those pertaining to sexual abuse and assault in detention facilities
ICE Health Service Corps	• Provides direct detainee care in some facilities, where corps members may serve as first responders in instances of sexual abuse and assault, and oversees care administered by non-ICE Health Services Corps providers in other facilities
Office of Acquisition Management (OAQ)	• Negotiates and manages ICE contracts and agreements for detainee housing at detention facilities
Office of Inspector General	• Operates a hotline to which detainees can report sexual abuse and assault allegations • Has investigative primacy for all sexual abuse and assault allegations against DHS or contractor staff members regardless of how they are reported

DHS components and offices	Roles and responsibilities pertaining to SAAPI
Office for Civil Rights and Civil Liberties	• Investigates complaints alleging violation of civil rights and civil liberties and addresses allegations from a policy perspective • Consults with ICE in the development of detention standards, including SAAPI standards

Source: GAO analysis of DHS information.

[a]In May 2012, ICE issued guidance—Directive 11062.1: *Sexual Abuse and Assault Prevention and Intervention*—assigning SAAPI responsibilities to individual ICE components. This table focuses on the primary ICE offices and components with roles and responsbilities related to SAAPI in detention facilities; however, the directive also assigns SAAPI-related responsbilities to certain other offices, such as ICE's Homeland Security Investigations, which may take aliens into custody through arrest.

ICE Sexual Abuse and Assault Allegations Data Are Not Complete, Which Could Limit Their Usefulness for Detention Management

ICE Data Describe the Type and Outcome of Sexual Abuse and Assault Allegations, but Missing Data Could Limit Their Usefulness for Managing Abuse Prevention and Intervention

Our analysis of ICE JICMS data showed 215 allegations of sexual abuse and assault in ICE detention facilities from October 2009 through March 2013, during which time ICE data indicate that its detention facilities had more than 1.2 million admissions.[29] JICMS data describe the circumstances around the alleged incidents reported to OPR, and our analysis of these data showed that more sexual abuse and assault allegations were made against other detainees than against facility staff, and allegations against staff were most often related to actions taken while staff were conducting job duties. Specifically, our analysis showed that of the 215 allegations, 123 were allegations against fellow detainees

---

[29]JICMS is a system to log, track, and manage cases for all OPR functions including investigations, management inspections, and personnel security. Several groups within DHS use and access JICMS, including ICE, U.S. Customs and Border Protection, the Joint Intake Center, and the DHS OIG. There were an additional 9 allegations from this time period in JICMS for which OPR investigations remained open as of August 2013. We excluded these allegations from our analysis.

or inmates, 86 were allegations against staff members, and 6 did not specify the perpetrator.[30] In general, allegations that named fellow detainees as the perpetrator tended to be allegations of inappropriate touching or penetration or attempted penetration. Allegations that named staff members as the perpetrator tended to be allegations of harassment or allegations that a staff member had sexually abused the victim during the course of job duties—for example, by touching a detainee inappropriately during a pat-down search. Table 4 describes allegations reported in JICMS from October 2009 through March 2013.

---

[30]Between October 2009 and March 2013, OPR changed the definition of sexual abuse and assault it used to identify such allegations in JICMS. Specifically, prior to May 2012, OPR defined detainee-on-detainee sexual abuse or assault as one or more detainees engaging in, or attempting to engage in, a sexual act with another detainee or the use of threats, intimidation, inappropriate touching, or other actions or communications by one or more detainees aimed at coercing or pressuring another detainee to engage in a sexual act. Staff-on-detainee sexual abuse or assault was defined as a staff member engaging in, or attempting to engage in, a sexual act with any detainee or the intentional touching of a detainee's genitalia, anus, groin, breast, inner thigh, or buttocks with the intent to abuse, humiliate, harass, degrade, arouse, or gratify the sexual desires of any person. In addition staff sexual misconduct included profane or abusive language or gestures and inappropriate visual surveillance of detainees. In May 2012, OPR began to employ the sexual abuse and assault definition included in the 2011 PBNDS, which broadened detainee-on-detainee abuse to include *attempted* sexually abusive contact as well as intentional touching of a detainee in the same ways as previously defined by staff-on-detainee abuse when accomplished by force, coercion, or intimidation. The 2011 PBNDS staff-on-detainee abuse definition was broadened to also include repeated oral statements or comments of a sexual nature to a detainee, including demeaning references to gender, derogatory comments about body or clothing, or profane or obscene language or gestures.

Table 4: Characteristics of the 215 Closed Sexual Abuse and Assault Allegations at Immigration Detention Facilities Included in the Joint Integrity Case Management System, October 2009-March 2013, by Percentage

	Allegations against staff members[a]	Allegations against fellow detainees and inmates	Allegations against unspecified perpetrators	All allegations
Gender of alleged perpetrator				
Male	52	73	17	63
Female	23	19	0	20
Not specified	24	8	83	17
Type of abuse alleged				
Penetration/attempted penetration	13	25	17	20
Inappropriate touching	20	50	33	37
Harassment, including voyeurism	23	11	0	15
Part of staff duties[b]	34	Not applicable	0	13
Other or not specified	10	15	50	14

Source: GAO analysis of Joint Integrity Case Management System data.

Notes: Percentages do not sum to 100 because of rounding.

[a]This column includes 2 allegations that identified both staff and detainee perpetrators.

[b]This category includes alleged abuse and assault by staff during their employment duties, such as inappropriately touching a detainee during a pat-down search.

Of the 215 investigations of the allegations completed between October 2009 and March 2013, our analysis showed that 55 percent of the allegations were determined to be unsubstantiated (investigators could not determine if abuse had occurred), 38 percent unfounded (investigators determined that abuse had not occurred), and 7 percent—or 15 allegations—substantiated (investigators determined that abuse had occurred).[31] Substantiated allegations included both allegations against staff members and allegations against fellow detainees as well as a variety of types of sexual abuse and assault, including attempted penetration, inappropriate touching, and sexual harassment (for descriptions of the 15 substantiated allegations, see app. II). Nearly all of the detainees (51 of 53) we interviewed at the 9 facilities we visited housing detainees stated that they felt safe at the detention facility in

---

[31]Investigations into these 215 allegations were conducted by local law enforcement agencies, OPR investigators, or DHS OIG investigators.

GAO-14-38 Immigration Detention

which they were residing, which they attributed to factors such as respectful treatment and professionalism by guards and a peaceful culture among detainees.[32] Table 5 shows the outcomes of the 215 closed investigations of the sexual abuse and assault allegations.

Table 5: Results of Closed Investigations into Sexual Abuse and Assault Allegations Included in the Joint Integrity Case Management System, October 2009-March 2013

Outcome	Description	Number of investigations	Percentage of investigations
Substantiated	An investigation determined the alleged incident occurred.	15	7
Unsubstantiated	An investigation could not determine whether or not the alleged incident occurred.	119	55
Unfounded	An investigation determined that the alleged incident did not occur.	81	38

Source: GAO analysis of Joint Integrity Case Management System data.

Our analysis of the closing reports for these 215 investigations indicated several frequently cited reasons why the majority of allegations could not be proved or disproved and were therefore reported as unsubstantiated. For example, in 29 percent of the unsubstantiated allegations, our analysis showed that the alleged victim either chose not to cooperate with the investigation or recanted or denied the allegation. Detainees may also report false allegations—for example, in an attempt to delay deportation—according to officials at the facilities we visited. In addition, as DOJ has reported, confined individuals, including detainees, may not report sexual abuse and assault because doing so requires them to relive an experience that was traumatic, they feel shame or embarrassment about the incident, or they live in fear of retribution or retaliation from the perpetrator.[33] Therefore the extent to which data describing reported incidents reflect the actual incident rate is unknown. Other frequently cited reasons from our analysis were that no evidence of assault existed and local law enforcement or prosecutors chose not to pursue the case.[34]

---

[32]These results cannot be generalized across all detainees in all immigration detention facilities.

[33]Department of Justice, Regulatory Impact Assessment for PREA Final Rule, (2012), 39.

[34]According to OPR officials, local law enforcement or prosecutors may choose to decline a case for reasons such as insufficient evidence or higher-priority cases.

Less frequently cited reasons were that witness statements, medical evidence, or video evidence did not corroborate the allegation. Table 6 shows our analysis of the number and percentage of closing reports citing reasons for unsubstantiated allegations.

Table 6: GAO Analysis of Reasons Why 119 Sexual Abuse and Assault Allegations Reported in the Joint Integrity Case Management System Were Determined to Be Unsubstantiated, October 2009-March 2013

Reason[a]	Number of cases	Percentage of cases
Investigation did not uncover evidence that substantiated an assault.	46	39
Victim did not cooperate with the investigation, declined to press charges, or recanted the allegation.	35	29
Federal or local authorities chose not to pursue the case.	31	26
Incident occurred, but was determined not to constitute sexual abuse or assault.	12	10
Video surveillance footage did not corroborate allegation.	10	8
Medical evidence did not corroborate allegation.	6	5
Witness statements did not corroborate allegations.	10	8
Other reason provided, such as the alleged victim being deported.	30	25
No reason provided.	9	8

Source: GAO analysis of Joint Integrity Case Management System data.

[a]Some closing reports cite multiple reasons for the investigation outcome. Therefore, the total does not sum to 119, and percentages do not add to 100.

Allegations of sexual abuse and assault have not been consistently reported for entry into ICE's JICMS, and while ICE has issued guidance to help improve reporting, developing internal controls to monitor reporting could help ICE ensure that it has more complete allegations data moving forward. ICE detention standards require that facilities provide detainees with several methods to report sexual abuse and assault, and all ICE components are required to report any allegations they receive to the Joint Intake Center at OPR headquarters, which then is to open a case in JICMS.[35] In addition, the OIG and Office for Civil Rights and Civil Liberties also report certain allegations they receive to

---

[35]ICE, Directive 11062.1.

the Joint Intake Center or directly to ICE OPR.[36] These reporting methods include the fact that detainees can report abuse or assault to any facility or ERO staff member orally or in writing; and that detainees can make free phone calls to DHS headquarters hotlines, their consulates, and other pro bono services (for more information about the reporting and investigation process, see app. III). Most sexual abuse and assault allegations are reported by detainees to local facility management, rather than through headquarters hotlines or other mechanisms. For example, approximately three-quarters of the allegations contained in JICMS for October 2009 through March 2013 (163 of 215) were reported locally at a detention facility. When facility staff learn of an allegation, they are to report it to the local ERO field office, which is to officially report the allegation to the Joint Intake Center by submitting a Significant Incident Report.

However, we found examples of allegations reported locally by detainees, either to facilities or ERO field offices, from fiscal years 2010 through 2012, that were not included in JICMS because ERO field offices did not consistently report allegations they received to the Joint Intake Center.[37] In particular, 28 of the 70 allegations (40 percent) provided to us by ERO field office officials at the 10 facilities we visited for fiscal years 2010 through 2012 were not in JICMS, and these officials reported that they had not submitted Significant Incident Reports for them for reasons including that they deemed the allegation to constitute harassment rather

---

[36]According to OPR officials, if a detainee or third party reports an allegation directly to the DHS OIG and the OIG decides to investigate, the OIG would not report the allegation to the Joint Intake Center; however, if the OIG decides not to investigate, the OIG is to report the allegation to ICE. According to OIG officials, they rarely investigate sexual abuse and assault allegations in detention facilities. In particular, DHS Management Directive 0810.1, which establishes DHS policy regarding the DHS OIG, specifies that any allegation that the OIG chooses not to investigate is to be forwarded to the appropriate DHS component, which is OPR for allegations of sexual abuse and assault in detention facilities. According to the Office for Civil Rights and Civil Liberties officials, the office first refers allegations it receives to the DHS OIG, which generally declines and returns them to the Office for Civil Rights and Civil Liberties, after which the Office for Civil Rights and Civil Liberties investigates them or refers them to ICE OPR. Cases that the Office for Civil Rights and Civil Liberties refers to OPR are to be entered in JICMS.

[37]We limited our analysis of the extent to which these allegations appear in JICMS data to fiscal years 2010 through 2012 because these years of data were available at the time of our 10 site visits to detention facilities.

than abuse, or that they determined that the allegation was unfounded.[38] As a result, these 28 allegations were not included in ICE sexual abuse and assault data for that time period, although they were required to be reported to the Joint Intake Center, according to ICE officials responsible for JICMS data.[39] In May 2012, ICE issued a directive to establish policies and procedures for the prevention of sexual abuse or assault of individuals in ICE custody that clarified the requirement to report all sexual abuse and assault allegations to the Joint Intake Center.[40] According to the ICE Prevention of Sexual Assault coordinator, this directive, along with subsequent training ICE provided to ERO officials on its implementation, was intended to improve the reporting and completeness of sexual abuse and assault data captured in JICMS. This is a positive step that could help improve the reporting of sexual abuse and assault allegations by local ERO officials. However, OPR has not developed controls to ensure that ERO field office officials responsible for overseeing all facilities are reporting sexual abuse and assault allegations, and ERO field office officials told us that they did not submit Significant Incident Reports for 3 of 9 sexual abuse or assault allegations made after May 2012 at the facilities we visited.[41] According to OPR officials, ODO risk-based inspections, which we discuss in more detail later in this report, may help ensure that ICE ERO field office officials responsible for overseeing facilities ODO inspects report all sexual abuse and assault allegations to the Joint Intake Center. However, ODO inspected compliance with SAAPI provisions at a minority of facilities—an average of less than 8 (3 percent) from fiscal years 2010 through 2013—and OPR has not implemented controls to ensure reporting by field office officials at the remainder of facilities.

---

[38]For an additional 9 allegations, although ERO field office officials told us that they did not submit a Significant Incident Report for the allegation, OPR located the allegation in JICMS, indicating that ICE headquarters learned of the allegations through another DHS office or a third party.

[39]ICE initially communicated this requirement to ERO field office directors in a June 2006 memo titled *Protocol on Reporting and Tracking of Assaults*.

[40]ICE, Directive 11062.1.

[41]These 3 allegations consisted of 1 allegation that OPR could not locate in JICMS and 2 allegations for which ERO field office officials said that they did not submit Significant Incident Reports. While field office officials reported the latter 2 allegations by electronic mail to the Joint Intake Center or through the local OPR field office, they did not do so in accordance with ICE Directive 11062.1, which requires that the local ERO field office director submit a Significant Incident Report within 24 hours of an allegation.

Standards for Internal Control in the Federal Government highlights the need for capturing information to meet program objectives and determining that relevant, reliable, and timely information is available for management decision-making purposes.[42] Without complete data on sexual abuse and assault allegations at immigration detention facilities, ICE does not have all pertinent information needed for detention management decision making. In the past, ICE has used JICMS primarily to oversee investigations of individual allegations. However, according to agency officials, ICE plans to use reported sexual abuse allegations maintained in JICMS for incident review and monitoring as well.[43] The ICE May 2012 directive describes requirements for data use including that the ICE Prevention of Sexual Assault coordinator analyze and report on sexual abuse allegations, identify problem areas and recommend corrective actions for the agency, and provide an assessment of the agency's progress in addressing sexual abuse and assault in a publicly available annual report.[44] The DHS PREA notice of proposed rulemaking also proposes to require that ICE collect and aggregate data related to sexual abuse and assault to facilitate the agency's ability to detect possible patterns and help prevent future incidents. Developing and implementing additional controls to ensure reporting of sexual abuse and assault allegations by ERO field offices to the Joint Intake Center could help better ensure the completeness of JICMS sexual abuse and assault data and thereby strengthen these data's usefulness for making detention management decisions and meeting these program management goals.

---

[42]GAO/AIMD-00-21.3.1.

[43]In addition, DHS used JICMS sexual abuse data in the regulatory impact analysis accompanying DHS's notice of proposed rulemaking to identify a benchmark level of sexual abuse allegations and estimate the number of incidents at DHS confinement facilities. See DHS, *Standards to Prevent, Detect, and Respond to Sexual Abuse and Assault in Confinement Facilities: Initial Regulatory Impact Analysis* (2012), 24-26.

[44]ICE, Directive 11062.1.

ICE Is Working to Minimize Barriers to Detainees Reporting Abuse, but Certain Barriers Could Result in Unreported Allegations

According to ICE officials, ICE detention standards are intended to encourage detainees to report sexual abuse and assault and require facilities to provide multiple methods to report abuse; however, ICE data on sexual abuse allegations could also be incomplete because of barriers detainees sometimes face in reporting abuse.[45] The National Prison Rape Elimination Commission reported that efforts to enhance reporting depend on the accessibility and safety of mechanisms to report sexual abuse, and agencies should make reporting sexual abuse as easy, private, and secure as possible, including by providing detainees access to the DHS OIG and other hotlines. Further, according to the National Prison Rape Elimination Commission, some confined individuals, including detainees, will never feel comfortable reporting abuse internally to a corrections employee, and thus it is important to provide them with the option of confidentially reporting to an outside entity. Nearly all detainees we interviewed at 9 facilities (46 of 50) reported that they knew of at least one mechanism to report sexual abuse; however, some detainees (7 of 53) expressed concerns with reporting abuse, such as fear of retaliation or uncertainty that the allegation would be treated with confidentiality.[46] ICE has taken steps intended to help improve the reporting of sexual abuse and assault allegations by, for example, explicitly forbidding retaliation for reporting sexual abuse and assault in its detention standards, establishing a hotline to serve as an alternative method for detainees to report sexual abuse and assault to ICE headquarters, and appointing an agency-wide Prevention of Sexual Assault coordinator to oversee efforts to improve prevention and response practices, including with respect to reporting issues.

During our site visits to 10 facilities and review of phone records from approximately 200 detention facilities, we observed indications that detainees may sometimes face barriers to accessing the DHS OIG hotline for reporting abuse at some of the facilities we visited. Although detainees report most sexual abuse and assault allegations to local facility management, consistent with the National Prison Rape Elimination Commission's recommendations to facilitate reporting by detainees who may feel uncomfortable reporting internally, ICE requires that detainees at

---

[45]See appendix IV for more information about SAAPI provisions included in ICE detention standards.

[46]We interviewed 53 detainees at 9 facilities. Of these, 3 detainees at 3 facilities did not state whether they knew of at least one mechanism to report sexual abuse.

all facilities have access to make free phone calls to the OIG to report abuse, including sexual abuse and assault allegations. During our site visits, we attempted to connect to the OIG hotline using phones in detainee housing pods and had mixed success in reaching the hotline. Specifically, in 5 out of 19 total attempts using phones at 10 facilities, we were unable to reach the OIG hotline (4 instances) or were unable to leave a message for the OIG (1 instance). We were unable to determine if the problem was with the phone or the OIG hotline itself. We previously reported in 2007 that systematic problems in facility telephone systems restricted detainees' abilities to reach the OIG hotline and other pro bono numbers.[47] Specifically, we found that from November 2005 through November 2006, the percentage of unsuccessful calls placed to pro bono numbers programmed into ICE's telephone system ranged from approximately 26 percent to 65 percent each month, and that system-wide facility success rates for complete calls showed a similar trend of performance. We made seven recommendations to ensure that detainees could access resources by telephone and that all detainee complaints were reviewed and acted upon as necessary. DHS implemented these recommendations by monitoring a new contractor for the telephones, posting pro bono numbers in detainee housing areas, and testing facility telephones, among other actions. Our review of phone records data maintained by ERO's phone services contractor for fiscal years 2010 through 2012 showed that approximately 14 percent of calls placed to the OIG hotline by detainees from about 210 facilities were not connected, primarily because of detainees ending the call prior to its completion or the OIG hotline not answering the call.

OIG officials were able to provide a possible reason for why we were not able to leave a voice message on the hotline from one telephone, but did not know why calls placed to the hotline were not connected in four of our attempted calls and as shown by phone records data. According to OIG officials, the OIG hotline is not staffed with a live operator, but permits detainees to leave voice recordings, which OIG staff members are to listen to and document. These OIG officials explained that we may not have been able to leave a voice recording on the OIG hotline because the voice recording mailbox was full because of an OIG staffing shortage. More specifically, the OIG hotline voice recording mailbox can hold 135

---

[47]GAO, *Alien Detention Standards: Telephone Access Problems Were Pervasive at Detention Facilities; Other Deficiencies Did Not Show a Pattern of Noncompliance,* GAO-07-875 (Washington D.C.: July 6, 2007).

voice messages, after which the hotline does not permit callers to leave voice recordings. According to OIG officials, OIG staff are to empty the mailbox every day, but during staffing shortages, the mailbox may remain full. For example, OIG officials stated that the OIG experienced a staffing shortage from late May 2013 to late June 2013. OIG officials said that this staffing shortage has been resolved, but were unaware that the OIG could monitor hotline availability to detainees through connectivity data collected by ERO's phone services contractor. OIG officials stated that receiving data on connectivity issues would be helpful to monitor the ability of detainees to successfully call the OIG hotline from detention facilities. *Standards for Internal Control in the Federal Government* calls for information to be communicated to individuals within an entity who need it and in a form and within a time frame that enables the individuals to carry out their responsibilities.[48] OIG and ERO coordination to ensure OIG access to OIG hotline connectivity data could better ensure that the OIG has information it needs to identify and address any technical issues detainees face in reaching the OIG hotline. Receiving these data could also help better position the OIG to fulfill its responsibility under the Inspector General Act of 1978, as amended, to receive and review complaints and information from any source alleging abuses of civil rights and civil liberties by DHS employees and employees of DHS contractors.[49]

Detainees may also face confusion in how to contact the OIG hotline given that the navigation required to place a call to the hotline within the telephone system generally requires several steps, or may not leave sufficient information on the OIG hotline voice mail system, according to DHS officials. For example, these officials explained that detainees may not leave their names or the name of the facility in which they are confined in their voice mail message, which makes it difficult for ICE to take action on the allegation.

ICE officials acknowledged that there have been difficulties with detainees connecting to the OIG hotline from detention centers and stated that ICE established an alternative ICE-run hotline—the Community and Detainee Helpline—in February 2013 that detainees can

---

[48]GAO/AIMD-00-21.3.1.

[49]Pub. L. No. 95-452, § 8I(f)(1)(B), 92 Stat. 1101, *added by* Intelligence Reform and Terrorism Prevention Act of 2004, Pub. L. No. 108-458, § 8304, 118 Stat. 3638, 3868.

use to directly report sexual abuse and assault allegations to ICE.[50] According to ICE officials, the Community and Detainee Helpline—which is staffed with live operators for 12 hours each day—receives approximately 150 to 250 calls each day, over 60 percent of which pertain to detained individuals, and as of September 2013, had received a total of 83 calls concerning physical or sexual abuse.

Investigative Files Maintained at Facilities Varied in Completeness, Potentially Limiting Their Usefulness in Monitoring and Analyzing Sexual Abuse and Assault at Individual Facilities

Files documenting investigations of sexual abuse and assault at the 10 facilities we visited varied in the extent to which they contained complete documentation of the investigation and outcomes. OPR tracks sexual abuse and assault allegations reported to ICE headquarters via JICMS; however, individual facilities are responsible for maintaining investigative files for allegations of incidents occurring in those facilities. ICE detention standards specify that facilities are to document and track incidents of sexual abuse and assault in order to monitor, evaluate, and assess the effectiveness of the facility's SAAPI program. In particular, ICE detention standards specify that facilities are to maintain investigative files for sexual abuse allegations to include information such as incident and investigative reports, medical forms, and supporting memorandums, among other things.[51] Internal control standards state that management is responsible for developing detailed policies and procedures to fit the agency's operations, and according to ERO officials, these files should demonstrate that an investigation was complete and thorough. Further, federal internal control standards call for agencies to capture information needed to meet program objectives and determine that relevant, reliable, and timely information is available for decision making.[52]

Our review of the facilities' investigative files for all 70 allegations of sexual abuse and assault occurring from fiscal years 2010 through 2012 at the 10 facilities we visited, however, showed that the files did not consistently document and track information supporting the investigation of the sexual abuse incidents. Specifically, our review showed that these

---

[50]The Community and Detainee Helpline is available at all detention facilities authorized to hold detainees for more than 72 hours, according to ICE officials.

[51]ICE facilities subject to the 2007 Residential Standards, 2008 PBNDS, and 2011 PBNDS are required to adhere to these standards for investigative files; however, facilities under the 2000 NDS are not required to adhere to these standards.

[52]GAO/AIMD-00-21.3.1.

investigative files generally contained narrative information pertaining to the circumstances of the allegation; however, they varied in the extent to which they contained supporting documents, such as police reports and the outcome of the investigations. We conducted a more detailed analysis of the investigative files for a nonprobability sample of 15 of the 70, including at least 1 allegation file from each of the 9 facilities we visited at which there were allegations from fiscal years 2010 through 2012. Of the 15 files we reviewed in more detail, 9 files from 5 facilities did not include supporting documentation, and 8 files from 5 facilities did not include information about the outcomes of the investigation.[53] According to ICE officials and facility administrators, the files may be incomplete because ICE guidance does not provide facility officials with a clear understanding of what specific information they should include, or the missing documentation—such as the results of the forensic medical examination—is retained by another department within the facility, such as the medical clinic, among other things.

According to the ICE Prevention of Sexual Assault coordinator, information contained in facility files is important for SAAPI program management because it provides ICE with a basis to review how the facility responded to sexual abuse or assault allegations and a means for the facility's SAAPI program coordinator to determine how the facility could improve its response to allegations or to identify systemic or root causes of abuse. In addition, the DHS PREA notice of proposed rulemaking would establish requirements for facility investigations, which would apply to all facilities once the rule's standards are incorporated into facility contracts. The notice of proposed rulemaking proposes to require that facilities conduct a sexual abuse incident review at the conclusion of every investigation of sexual abuse and, where the allegation was not determined to be unfounded, prepare a written report recommending whether the allegation or investigation indicates that a change in policy or practice could better prevent, detect, or respond to sexual abuse, among other new requirements. By clarifying guidance to help ensure that ICE and facility administrators correctly document investigations into sexual abuse and assault allegations, ICE could better ensure the completeness

---

[53]Our more detailed analysis of the investigative files for these allegations identified files at a total of 8 facilities that did not include either supporting documentation or information about the outcomes of the investigation. ICE's contracts or agreements with 4 of these 8 facilities cited detention standards that included specific requirements for maintaining investigative files for sexual abuse allegations at the time the allegation was reported.

of facility files for SAAPI program management purposes and better position ICE and facility administrators to comply with the provisions of the DHS notice of proposed rulemaking.

Sexual Abuse and Assault Provisions in Detention Standards Vary in Content and Applicability across Facilities

Three of Four Sets of DHS Detention Standards Include Provisions Focused on Sexual Abuse and Assault

ICE has four sets of detention standards for facilities, three of which include provisions on SAAPI and one that does not include SAAPI provisions. Specifically, the 2000 NDS do not include such provisions, but the three sets of standards that ICE subsequently developed—the 2007 Family Residential Standards, the 2008 PBNDS, and the 2011 PBNDS—each include specific SAAPI provisions. The SAAPI provisions included in the standards have increased in number and breadth over time, as shown in table 7. The 2007 and 2008 standards include SAAPI provisions spanning various topical areas, such as written policies and procedures, program coordination, and investigation and prosecution. Most recently, ICE developed the 2011 PBNDS, which include SAAPI provisions that address the same topical areas as the 2008 PBNDS and are similarly intended to apply to adult facilities. However, the 2011 PBNDS include additional requirements, such as that written policies and procedures include statement of a zero-tolerance policy for all forms of sexual abuse or assault, and broader requirements within the topical areas, such as that intergovernmental service agreement facilities designate a SAAPI coordinator rather than only service processing centers and contract detention facilities. Appendix IV provides more detailed information about SAAPI provisions currently used across ICE detention standards for adult facilities.

Table 7: Examples of Sexual Abuse and Assault Prevention and Intervention (SAAPI) Provisions in U.S Immigration Customs and Enforcement (ICE) Detention Standards for Adult Facilities

Topical area	2000 National Detention Standards requirements	2008 Performance-Based National Detention Standards (PBNDS) requirements	Requirements in 2011 PBNDS beyond those in 2008 PBNDS
Written policies and procedures	None for SAAPI.	Require facility administrators to have written SAAPI policies and procedures.	Require written SAAPI policies and procedures to include additional components, such as a statement of a zero-tolerance policy for all forms of sexual abuse or assault.
Program coordination	None for SAAPI.	Require service processing centers and contract detention facilities to designate a SAAPI coordinator to, among other things, coordinate the gathering of reports on incidents of sexual abuse or assault.	Require all facilities that house detainees for more than 72 hours, including intergovernmental service agreement facilities, to designate a SAAPI coordinator.
Investigation and prosecution	Require facilities to develop a process for investigating detainee grievances, including allegations, but do not specifically address sexual abuse or assault investigations.	Stipulate that a sensitive and coordinated response is necessary when a detainee alleges sexual abuse or assault, and that all allegations are promptly and effectively investigated. Require that staff preserve the crime scene, when possible, and arrange for the victim to undergo a forensic medical examination, based on factors such as availability of in-house expertise and security considerations.	Require that all investigations into alleged sexual assault be prompt, thorough, objective, and conducted by trained investigators. In addition, the facility administrator must arrange for the victim to undergo an off-site forensic medical examination in all cases, rather than based on such factors as availability of in-house expertise and general security considerations. Also require the facility SAAPI coordinator to review the results of every investigation of sexual abuse to assess and improve prevention and response efforts.

Source: GAO analysis of ICE detention standards.

Note: The 2007 Family Residential Standards are not included in this table because the table focuses on facilities that generally house adult immigration detainees. The 2007 Family Residential Standards are intended to apply to facilities that house families, and as of August 2013, 1 of ICE's 251 detention facilities housed families.

SAAPI provisions in the DHS PREA notice of proposed rulemaking build on those included in the PBNDS and other DHS detention policies, and according to DHS officials, are similar to the provisions in the 2011 PBNDS, with certain differences. In addition, the provisions in the notice of proposed rulemaking in many respects incorporate the standards for immigration detention facilities recommended by the National Prison Rape Elimination Commission, as shown in appendix V. As a set of regulations, if finalized, DHS's PREA notice of proposed rulemaking would carry more legal weight than agency policy with respect to the roles and responsibilities of ICE employees.[54] DOJ's PREA rule, from which various provisions in DHS's notice of proposed rulemaking adopt exact language, with certain differences—such as content for sexual abuse training—applies to all facilities in a state, including state and local facilities under agreement with USMS that house ICE detainees.[55] Appendix VI provides examples of select differences between the standards included in DOJ's PREA rule and DHS's PREA notice of proposed rulemaking.

ICE Does Not Have Consistent and Reliable Information to Determine the Extent to Which Sexual Abuse and Assault Provisions Apply to Different Facilities

ICE has information regarding the detention standards and SAAPI provisions generally in place at different types of detention facilities; however, ICE does not have reliable information to identify which detention standards and SAAPI provisions apply to individual facilities. As discussed previously, ICE establishes the standards applicable to its detention facilities through either individual contracts or agreements. According to ICE officials and documentation, the SAAPI provisions cited in facility contracts or agreements vary by facility, but there are general patterns across facility types, as summarized in table 8. ICE detention program officials explained that not all facilities are bound to ICE's most recent standards because of resource considerations. In particular, if facilities that house very few detainees require additional funds to adopt more recent standards, it might not be cost-effective for ICE to

---

[54]Provisions in the rule that are applicable to ICE would be effective on the date a final version of the rule takes effect and would carry more legal weight than agency policy for ICE and ICE employees. Provisions in the rule that are applicable to facilities would be effective once they are incorporated into facility contracts and would therefore carry the same legal weight as the detention standards in existing contracts. 77 Fed. Reg. at 75,304.

[55]State-controlled facilities, including USMS intergovernmental agreement facilities, that do not implement the DOJ PREA rule may cause state forfeiture of DOJ grant funding. In particular, PREA provides that DOJ shall withhold 5 percent of prison-related grant funding from any state that fails to certify that it has adopted, and is in full compliance with, DOJ's PREA standards or that fails to provide an assurance that not less than 5 percent of the relevant grant funding shall be used to enable the state to adopt, and achieve full compliance with, DOJ's PREA standards toward future certification. See 42 U.S.C. 15607(c)(2). Under DOJ's PREA rule, the state's certification that it is in full compliance with the PREA standards applies to all facilities under the operational control of the state's executive branch, including facilities operated by private entities on behalf of the state's executive branch. See 28 C.F.R. § 115.501. DOJ's PREA rule therefore does not contain noncompliance sanctions for county intergovernmental agreement facilities that fail to adopt or implement DOJ's PREA standards. See 77 Fed. Reg. at 37,115.

renegotiate the contract or agreement. ICE detention program and contracting officials also stated that, in general, the agency is prioritizing modifications of contracts or agreements to first implement the 2011 PBNDS at facilities that exclusively house ICE detainees and that house the greatest number of detainees—service processing centers, contract detention facilities, and dedicated intergovernmental service agreement facilities.

Table 8: Sexual Abuse and Assault Prevention and Intervention (SAAPI) Provisions Applicable to Immigration Detention Facilities, as of August 2013

Facility type	Detention standards generally applicable to facility type, according to U.S. Immigration and Customs Enforcement (ICE) officials and documentation	Average percentage of detainee population, fiscal years 2010-2012[a]
Service processing center	2011 Performance-Based National Detention Standards (PBNDS). All service processing centers have signed contract modifications adopting the 2011 PBNDS in full.	12
Contract detention facility	2011 PBNDS. All contract detention facilities have signed contract modifications adopting the 2011 PBNDS in full.	19
Dedicated intergovernmental service agreement	2007 Family Residential Standards, 2008 PBNDS, or 2011 PBNDS. All but 2 of the dedicated intergovernmental service agreement facilities have signed contract modifications specifically adopting the 2011 PBNDS SAAPI provisions, but not the 2011 PBNDS pertaining to other topical areas.[b]	22
Nondedicated intergovernmental service agreement	2000 National Detention Standards, 2008 PBNDS, or 2011 PBNDS. In 2012, ICE sent letters to the 53 nondedicated intergovernmental service agreement facilities that house detainees for more than 72 hours and have average daily populations of more than 10 detainees requesting that they sign contract modifications to specifically adopt the 2011 PBNDS SAAPI provisions. As of August 2013, 37 facilities had signed a modification.	34
Family residential	2007 Family Residential Standards	<1
U.S. Marshals Service intergovernmental agreement or contract	U.S. Marshals Service intergovernmental agreement and contract facilities are not generally required to adhere to ICE SAAPI provisions. However, these facilities are to adhere to the Department of Justice's (DOJ) final Prison Rape Elimination Act of 2003 (PREA) rule.	14

Source: GAO analysis of ICE testimony and documentation.

[a]Percentages do not sum to 100 because of rounding.

[b]ICE classifies 1 of the 2 facilities that had not signed a contract modification as a family residential facility, but it is considered a dedicated intergovernmental service agreement facility for the purpose of this report because it was converted to a women-only facility in 2009 and no longer houses families. The 2 facilities that had not signed a contract modification, but were governed by the SAAPI provisions included in the 2007 Residential Standards or 2008 PBNDS, housed an average of 4 percent of the total detainee population from fiscal years 2010 through 2012.

ICE headquarters and ERO field office officials do not have consistent and reliable information readily available on which detention standards—and the SAAPI provisions they contain—apply to which individual facilities. OAQ contracting officials maintain information on the applicable detention standards for ICE's detention facilities, but this information was not fully consistent with ICE contracts and agreements with those facilities. OAQ headquarters officials provided us with a spreadsheet listing their understanding of standards cited in ICE's contracts and agreements with detention facilities; however, when we reviewed detention standards listed in this spreadsheet against the standards listed in a sample of 20 facility contracts and agreements, the standards listed in the spreadsheet were not consistent with the facility contracts and agreements for almost half (9) of these facilities.[56] According to OAQ officials, OAQ retains ICE contracts and agreements with detention facilities in electronic files, but does not have a central system in which all contract and agreement documentation is stored. OAQ officials explained that in 2012 OAQ's four regional divisions, each of which oversees detention contracts and agreements for facilities in a different area within the United States, manually reviewed ICE's contracts and agreements with its 251 facilities and recorded the detention standards cited in a spreadsheet. OAQ reviewed and updated this spreadsheet to furnish us with information on the standards cited in ICE's contracts and agreements with detention facilities, and according to OAQ officials, it may have missed some changes that occurred since it initially developed the spreadsheet. However, the standards in the contracts and agreements for facilities for which inconsistent information was recorded did not change within the last year. During the course of our audit work, OAQ officials corrected the data inconsistencies we identified through our review of the sample of 20 contracts and agreements; however, without checking its data for the remaining 231 facilities, OAQ does not have reasonable assurance that its data are consistent and reliable.

We also requested that ERO headquarters provide us with information about the standards governing each detention facility, and found discrepancies between facility contracts and agreements and ERO's data. In particular, ERO detention program officials provided us with the data they maintain on detention standards—a listing of the detention standards under which ERO inspects each facility—that they extracted from the

---

[56]We selected this sample to include (1) facilities at which we conducted site visits and (2) facilities for which ERO and OAQ information on facility standards differed.

Facility Performance Management System.[57] However, the detention standards cited for 8 of the same sample of 20 facilities for which we reviewed contract and agreement documentation were inconsistent. We also observed differences between information maintained by OAQ and ERO, in that OAQ and ERO recorded different standards in their spreadsheets or in information on facilities' standards that they subsequently provided for 10 facilities.[58] ERO headquarters officials attributed one discrepancy between the contracts and agreements and ERO's data to an error in the Facility Performance Management System—a relatively new system released in June 2012—that was in the final stages of testing during our review.

In addition, ICE officials stated that ERO's data reflect the standards under which ERO inspects facilities rather than those cited in the facility contracts or agreements, and that ERO performs inspections under standards that are more rigorous than those cited in its contracts and agreements with some facilities. In particular, according to ERO officials, at facilities at which the 2000 NDS are cited in the contracts or agreements, ERO field office officials responsible for overseeing the facilities, or the administrators operating the facilities, may request that inspections be completed under the 2008 PBNDS because they believe the facilities are exceeding 2000 NDS requirements and want that formally confirmed through inspections. In such instances, ERO generally inspects the facilities under the more rigorous standards, according to ERO officials. A senior ICE official responsible for detention policy explained that ERO inspecting a facility under more rigorous standards than those cited in the facility's contract or agreement is acceptable with agreement from the facility, and can be beneficial to ICE because it permits the agency to hold facilities accountable for more rigorous requirements. For example, by inspecting a facility with a contract that cites the 2000 NDS under the 2008 PBNDS, ERO is able to hold the facility accountable for SAAPI provisions that would not be required of the facility if it were inspected under the 2000 NDS, which do not include SAAPI provisions. In addition, this senior official stated that it can be more

---

[57]The Facility Performance Management System is a database for identifying and providing access to detention inspection information and facilitating the production and maintenance of facility analytics and reporting.

[58]We included the contracts for these 10 facilities in the sample of 20 contracts we reviewed.

efficient and cost-effective for ICE to ensure that facilities adhere to more rigorous standards through the inspection process rather than modifying the facilities' contracts or agreements to include the more rigorous standards because, for example, facilities may request to open negotiations for the entire contract and request additional funding from ICE.

At the field level, we observed that ICE field office and facility program officials overseeing 5 of the 10 facilities we visited did not have reliable information about the standards cited in their contracts or agreements with ICE. In particular, ERO DSM and field office officials at 2 of the 10 facilities asserted that the facility's contract or agreement cited the 2008 PBNDS when its contract cited the 2000 NDS. ERO field office officials at 3 additional facilities stated that the facility had signed a contract modification adopting the 2011 PBNDS SAAPI provisions when it had not, or vice versa.[59] ERO field office officials attributed these inconsistencies to factors such as OAQ providing them with inaccurate information and interpreting the language about detention standards included in the contract differently from OAQ headquarters officials.[60]

Inconsistent information about the detention standards cited in facilities' contracts or agreements can affect facility owners' and administrators' understanding of their responsibilities to ICE and the information available to decision makers and stakeholders regarding the standards applicable to the facilities. Our review of ICE facility inspection reports from fiscal years 2010 through 2013, which we discuss in more detail later in this report, for the same sample of 20 facility contracts and agreements, showed that there were at least 10 instances at 2 facilities in which ERO or ICE's ODO assessed compliance with the 2008 PBNDS, including the SAAPI standard, when the facility was contractually bound to the 2000 NDS, which have no SAAPI standard. The administrators we spoke with

---

[59]DSM and ERO field office officials at the other 5 facilities we visited had accurate information about the standards to which the facilities they oversaw were contractually bound.

[60]Headquarters OAQ officials told us that when a contract or agreement states that the facility must perform in accordance with the most current edition of ICE's detention standards, it means that facilities must comply with whatever the most current standards were at the time the contract was signed; however, officials from one ERO field office interpreted this language to require compliance with standards issued after the contract was signed.

at these 2 facilities were unaware that they were contractually required to adhere to the 2000 NDS, not the 2008 PBNDS. According to ERO officials, ERO has not established a process for documenting that a facility administrator understands that the standards under which ERO is inspecting the administrator's facility exceed those required by the facility contract or agreement, or the facility administrator's consent to such an inspection in these instances. Nevertheless, ERO may discuss the issue and gain agreement with facility administrators by means such as electronic mail, according to ERO officials. These officials also stated that ERO can generally remove detainees from a facility if it does not comply with the standards under which ERO inspects the facility, even if those standards are more rigorous than those cited in the facilities' contracts and agreements, and thus it is not always imperative for inspection purposes for ERO to modify its contracts and agreements with facilities to incorporate the more rigorous standards.

Standards for Internal Control in the Federal Government calls for agencies to develop control activities to help ensure that data are accurately recorded and communicated to management and others within the entity who need them and specifies that all transactions and other significant events need to be clearly documented, and the documentation should be readily available for examination.[61] Documenting and maintaining reliable information on the detention standards cited in facilities' contracts and agreements with ICE, as well as recording any agreements by facilities to undergo inspection under more rigorous standards, could better position ICE headquarters officials, ERO field office officials, facility administrators, and other stakeholders, such as inspectors and auditors, to have a reliable and consistent understanding of applicable facility detention standards.

Reliable information on the SAAPI provisions cited in facilities' contracts or agreements could also help ICE better plan for the resources and time necessary to implement DHS's PREA rule. According to DHS's PREA notice of proposed rulemaking, once the rule is finalized, DHS would establish a process for requiring that all 126 detention facilities under an ICE contract or agreement (family residential facilities, service processing centers, contract detention facilities, ICE dedicated intergovernmental service agreement facilities, and ICE nondedicated intergovernmental

---

[61]GAO/AIMD-00-21.3.1.

service agreement facilities) comply with the final rule's SAAPI provisions.[62] In particular, according to the notice of proposed rulemaking, the proposed provisions would be phased in through the inclusion in new contracts and contract renewals of an obligation to adopt and comply with the provisions set forth in the final rule. Accordingly, the SAAPI provisions in the final rule would supersede the SAAPI provisions these 126 facilities currently have in place under the 2007 Residential Standards, 2008 PBNDS, or 2011 PBNDS, as well as establish SAAPI provisions at those facilities operating under the 2000 NDS that currently have no such provisions. According to OAQ officials, incorporating the provisions proposed in DHS's PREA notice of proposed rulemaking will likely take multiple years to complete. According to DHS, the department cannot be certain how much, if any, of the costs associated with implementation it will pay, as those costs will be determined through negotiation with facilities.[63] These costs could include, for example, staff training, providing detainees with access to outside confidential support services, and documentation of cross-gender pat-downs. Reliable baseline information about SAAPI provisions currently applicable to facilities, as established in their contracts and agreements with ICE, could help ICE estimate any costs associated with implementing the final DHS PREA rule that the department might incur during contract negotiations, and determine appropriate time frames for contract negotiations. Documenting and maintaining reliable information on the detention standards applicable to facilities across ICE components could better position ICE officials to have accurate information to effectively plan for program operations, such as the implementation of DHS's final PREA rule.

[62]DHS's proposed standards would not apply to the 125 USMS intergovernmental agreement facilities that house ICE detainees, which are governed by DOJ's PREA rule.

[63]See DHS, *Standards to Prevent, Detect, and Respond to Sexual Abuse and Assault in Confinement Facilities: Initial Regulatory Impact Analysis* (2012).

DHS Focused Its Sexual Abuse and Assault Oversight on Facilities Housing Most Detainees and Found Most Facilities Compliant with Provisions

ICE Used Various Oversight Methods to Assess Compliance with SAAPI Provisions at More than Half of Facilities That Housed About 90 Percent of Detainees

During fiscal years 2010 through 2013, ICE provided oversight of its three sets of SAAPI provisions at 157 of approximately 250 detention facilities that housed about 90 percent of ICE detainees. ICE officials said that they did not perform SAAPI oversight at the remaining facilities because they inspected the facilities under the 2000 NDS, which do not have SAAPI provisions.[64] In particular, ICE used four primary mechanisms for assessing facilities' compliance with SAAPI provisions: (1) annual inspections conducted by an ERO contractor, (2) periodic inspections by ODO personnel, (3) continuous ERO on-site monitoring provided by a DSM, and (4) annual self-assessments by certain facilities that passed two consecutive ERO inspections and met other requirements.[65] According to ICE officials responsible for facility oversight, these different oversight methods complement each other and serve different purposes. ERO inspections are to assess compliance with all standards across facilities and, according to ERO officials, ERO generally focuses on

---

[64]As previously discussed, ICE inspects certain facilities contractually bound to, or under agreement with, the 2000 NDS under the 2008 PBNDS.

[65]Specifically, ERO and ODO performed a total of 140 inspections at 42 facilities to directly assess SAAPI compliance from fiscal years 2010 through 2013. Of these 140 inspections, 134 were performed using the 2008 PBNDS SAAPI provisions, 4 were performed using the 2011 PBNDS SAAPI provisions, and 2 used the 2007 Family Residential Standards SAAPI provisions. Certain facilities started performing annual facility self-assessments in fiscal year 2012, and 93 facilities had completed self-assessments as of August 2013. In addition to passing two consecutive ERO inspections, eligible facilities (1) house detainees for less than 72 hours, or (2) house an average daily population of 10 detainees or fewer. ICE requires all facilities participating in the self-assessment program to comply with the 2011 SAAPI standard. According to ICE officials, prior to fiscal year 2012, ICE inspected these facilities under the NDS, which do not have a SAAPI standard.

performing inspections at facilities that that house 10 or more detainees.[66] ODO conducts more limited, but in-depth inspections of certain standards at facilities selected using a risk-based approach.[67] DSMs are to monitor facility adherence to ICE's detention standards on a day-to-day basis and provide facilities with technical guidance, including for implementing corrective action plans, as needed.

ICE used one or more oversight mechanisms to assess SAAPI compliance at certain facilities ERO identified as subject to the 2007 Family Residential Standards or the 2008 or 2011 PBNDS.[68] In fiscal year 2012, for example, ICE assessed compliance with SAAPI provisions at 61 facilities and used at least two oversight mechanisms at 28 of the 61 facilities at which it assessed SAAPI compliance (46 percent). These 28 facilities housed about 55 percent of ICE detainees in fiscal year 2012, as illustrated in figure 2.[69]

---

[66]These facilities also are to have a total of 60 or more man days, where a man day constitutes one night spent by one detainee. About 130 of ICE's approximately 250 detention facilities had an average daily detainee population of 10 or more detainees from fiscal years 2010 through 2012.

[67]According to ODO officials, ODO selects the facilities it inspects using a risk-based model that uses deficiencies identified in ERO's annual inspections, number and type of allegations, average daily detention population, deficiencies identified in prior ODO inspections, and date of last ODO inspection.

[68]According to ICE officials, in some instances a facility will request or agree to be inspected under a set of standards that is more rigorous than required by its contract or agreement toward demonstrating that it is exceeding its required standards. Therefore, a facility that is required by its contract or agreement to adhere to the 2000 NDS, which do not include a SAAPI standard, may be inspected under the 2008 or 2011 PBNDS, which include a SAAPI standard.

[69]ICE did not assess SAAPI compliance through inspections or the DSM program at facilities in the self-assessment program in fiscal year 2012.

Figure 2: U.S. Immigration and Customs Enforcement (ICE) Oversight Mechanisms That Included Sexual Abuse and Assault Oversight by Detention Facilities and Average Daily Detainee Population, Fiscal Year 2012

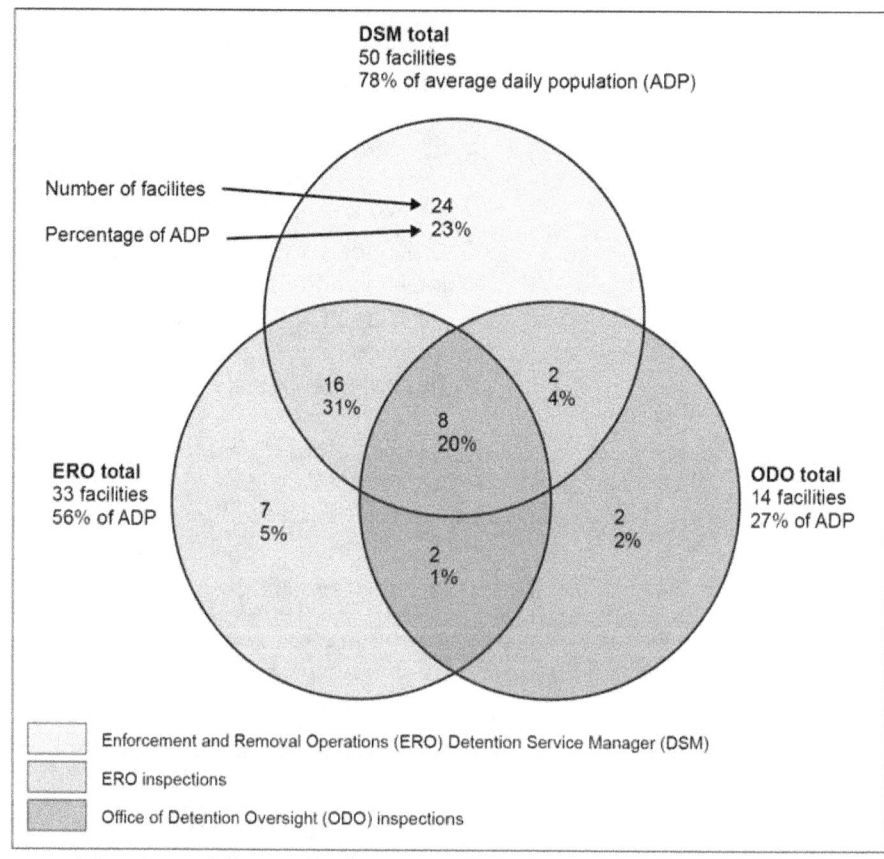

Source: GAO analysis of ICE documents.

Note: According to ERO officials, DSMs may monitor the reporting process of sexual abuse and assault allegations, regardless of inspection standards.

ICE Oversight Identified SAAPI-Related Deficiencies, but ERO Inspections Were Performed Inconsistently

ICE oversight of its three sets of SAAPI provisions from fiscal years 2010 through 2013 identified few deficiencies through ERO and ODO inspections, and ERO officials provided one example of a SAAPI deficiency identified through the DSM program. However, ERO's review of results from the first year of the self-assessment program identified deficiencies with SAAPI provisions at over a third of facilities. In addition, DOJ provides oversight related to preventing sexual abuse and assault at facilities under agreement with USMS that house detainees.

ERO Inspections

ERO identified few deficiencies in facility compliance with the 2008 or 2011 SAAPI provisions from fiscal years 2010 through 2013, and found 1 facility did not meet the overall 2011 SAAPI standard.[70] In particular, ERO inspections identified deficiencies during 11 of 110 inspections (10 percent) at 39 facilities. Most deficiencies (7 of 11) were in SAAPI priority provisions, such as the provision that staff be trained in required SAAPI areas.[71] Table 9 summarizes the deficiencies identified by the inspections ERO performed under the 2008 SAAPI provisions.

Table 9: Enforcement and Removal Operations (ERO) Inspection Results of the 2008 Performance-Based National Detention Standards Sexual Abuse and Assault Prevention and Intervention (SAAPI) Provisions, Fiscal Years 2010 through 2013

SAAPI standard provision	Meets standard	Does not meet standard	Not applicable
Applicable to contract detention facilities or service processing centers only			
For service processing centers and contract detention facilities, the written policy and procedure has been approved by the ERO field office director.	50	3	55
For service processing centers and contract detention facilities, the Sexual Assault Awareness Information brochure is available for detainees.[a]	78	1	29
Applicable to all detention facilities and related to sexual abuse and assault allegations			
Tracking statistics and reports are readily available for review by the inspectors.	78	1	29

[70]Our analysis included inspection reports available as of September 23, 2013. At that time, all but 2 inspection reports scheduled for fiscal year 2013 were available for our review. During this time period, ERO contractors performed nearly all inspections under the 2008 PBNDS (108 inspections at 39 facilities) and a few inspections under the 2011 PBNDS (2 inspections at 2 facilities). ERO did not perform any inspections under the 2007 Family Residential Standards during this time period. See appendix VII for the SAAPI provisions that constitute the overall SAAPI standard under the 2008 PBNDS and the 2011 PBNDS.

[71]According to ODPP officials, in March 2013 an ICE working group—composed of representatives from ERO, ODPP, and the Office for Civil Rights and Civil Liberties, among others—determined priority provisions within the 2008 and 2011 PBNDS. ICE considers these priority provisions to be of most critical importance within each detention standard based on significance to issues such as health and life safety, facility security, detainee rights, and quality of life in detention. See appendix VII for the SAAPI standard provisions ICE identified as priorities under the 2008 and 2011 PBNDS. ICE officials said that they may remove detainees from, or withhold payment to, a facility that fails to meet one of its priority standard provisions. These officials also said that ICE has not removed detainees or withheld payment based on SAAPI standard deficiencies.

SAAPI standard provision	Meets standard	Does not meet standard	Not applicable
All records associated with claims of sexual abuse or assault are maintained, and such incidents are specifically logged and tracked by a designated staff coordinator.	104	0	4
When there is an alleged sexual assault, staff conduct a thorough investigation, gather and maintain evidence, and make referrals to appropriate law enforcement agencies for possible prosecution.	106	0	2
Victims of sexual abuse or assault are referred to specialized community resources for treatment and gathering of evidence.	106	1	1
PRIORITY: There is prompt and effective intervention when any detainee is sexually abused or assaulted and there are policy and procedures for required chain-of-command reporting.	106	1	1
PRIORITY: When there is an alleged or proven sexual assault, the required notifications to U.S. Immigration and Customs Enforcement (ICE), facility management, and the appropriate law enforcement agency are promptly made.	107	0	1
Applicable to all detention facilities and otherwise related to sexual abuse and assault			
PRIORITY: All staff are trained, during orientation and in annual refresher training, in the prevention and intervention areas required by the SAAPI detention standard.	106	2	0
PRIORITY: Detainees are screened upon arrival for "high-risk" sexual assaultive and sexual victimization potential and housed and counseled accordingly. Detainees who are likely to become victims will be placed in the least restrictive housing that is available and appropriate.	106	2	0
PRIORITY: Detainees are informed about the program in facility orientation and the detainee handbook (or equivalent)	107	1	0
PRIORITY: The facility has a SAAPI program that includes, at a minimum: • measures to prevent sexual abuse and sexual assault, • Policy and procedures for required chain-of-command reporting to the highest facility official and the ICE field office director, • measures for prompt and effective intervention to address the safety and treatment needs of detainee victims if an assault occurs, and • investigation of incidents of sexual assault, and discipline assailants.	107	1	0
The Sexual Assault Awareness Notice is posted on all housing unit bulletin boards.[b]	108	0	0

Source: GAO analysis of ERO inspection reports.

Notes: Inspectors assessed the two provisions applicable only to contract detention facilities and service processing centers at 9 of 63 and 35 of 63 intergovernmental service agreement facilities, respectively, and did not assess them at one contract detention facility. Inspectors did not assess a facility to not meet the same SAAPI provision more than once during this time frame. One inspection determined that the facility did not meet multiple provisions.

[a]ICE's Sexual Assault Awareness Information brochure contains information on sexual abuse and assault definitions, avoiding sexual assault, and what to do if assaulted, among other things.

[b]The Sexual Assault Awareness Notice contains contact information for reporting sexual abuse and assault to a facility staff member, ICE officials, ICE's Community and Detainee Helpline, and ICE's Joint Intake Center.

In addition, of the 2 facilities inspected under the 2011 SAAPI provisions, 1 met all SAAPI provisions and 1 did not meet the overall SAAPI standard. ERO officials responsible for inspections explained that one way in which facilities do not meet an overall detention standard is if they do not meet three priority provisions within the standard.[72] The facility that did not meet the overall SAAPI standard did not meet 12 of the 21 applicable 2011 SAAPI provisions, including 6 priority provisions.[73] (See app. VII for all 2011 SAAPI provisions.) Our review of ERO corrective action plans showed that corrective actions were taken at 9 of the 11 facilities to address the SAAPI deficiencies the inspections identified in a manner consistent with ICE requirements.[74] ERO officials explained that they did not know why 1 facility did not take corrective actions within the required time frame to address these deficiencies, and that another facility did not do so because the facility and ERO determined that the 2011 PBNDS were too onerous for the size of the facility, facility resources, and ICE population housed at the facility, and that ERO would conduct a 90-day follow-up inspection under the 2008 PBNDS.

Our further review of 110 ERO inspection reports—108 assessing compliance with the 2008 SAAPI provisions and 2 with the 2011 SAAPI provisions—documenting performance at 39 facilities from fiscal years 2010 through 2013 showed that some inspection teams did not assess all appropriate 2008 SAAPI standard provisions, providing inconsistent information for detention oversight. In these inspection reports, inspectors are to use a worksheet specific to either the 2008 PBNDS or the 2011 PBNDS to document if a facility meets or does not meet each SAAPI standard provision, as well as if the provision does not apply to the

---

[72]In addition, according to ERO officials, inspectors may determine that a facility did not meet the overall SAAPI standard if the facility fails numerous nonpriority SAAPI provisions.

[73]ERO conducted this inspection in February 2013 as a preoccupancy inspection, at which time there were no ICE detainees at the facility. Since that time, this facility has housed an average of 2 detainees daily.

[74]According to ERO officials, starting in December 2010, ERO required the relevant ERO field office to take and report corrective actions identified by ERO or ODO inspections within 5 days for a deficiency in a priority standard, or 55 days for other deficiencies.

facility.[75] (See app. VII for a comparison of the 2008 and 2011 PBNDS SAAPI inspection worksheets.) We found that inspectors did not assess or collect information for all the 2008 SAAPI provisions at facilities where no sexual abuse or assault allegations were made during the time period under review; rather, the inspectors recorded that these provisions did not apply. In particular, inspectors did not assess during 29 of 108 inspections (27 percent) whether facilities met the provision to have sexual abuse statistics and reports readily available for review by inspectors and inspectors did not assess whether 4 facilities met the provision to maintain all records associated with claims of sexual abuse or assault. ERO officials said that inspectors should evaluate all SAAPI standard provisions at all inspected facilities, even if no sexual abuse or assault allegations were made; for example an inspector could still verify that the facility has a framework for tracking statistics, should allegations occur. ERO officials said that they orally communicated this expectation to the inspections contractor in March 2012.[76]

However, our review of inspections conducted after March 2012 found that inspectors continued to not assess or collect information for all applicable 2008 SAAPI standard provisions. Specifically, 4 of 43 inspections conducted from March 2012 through September 2013 did not assess or collect information for all applicable 2008 SAAPI standard provisions, including the provision to have sexual abuse statistics and reports readily available for review by inspectors (2 of 4), among others. Contractor representatives responsible for inspection oversight stated that they may not have assessed all 2008 SAAPI provisions because of inspector error. ERO officials responsible for inspection oversight stated that ERO has processes in place to ensure that contracted inspectors consistently inspect all SAAPI provisions, such as ERO field office personnel reviewing inspection results and system controls that assign a detention standard rating based on checkmarks in each provision. However, these processes would not identify instances when inspectors

---

[75]These worksheets vary according to detention standards. For example, the 2008 SAAPI standard worksheet contains 13 provisions, and the 2011 SAAPI standard worksheet contains 22 standard provisions. In addition, the inspectors can include remarks for every provision, regardless of whether the provision met the standard, did not meet the standard, or was not applicable.

[76]That is, with the exception of two SAAPI provisions that apply only to service processing centers and contract detention facilities highlighted in table 9, which are unrelated to the inconsistency we observed.

inaccurately determined that a SAAPI provision did not apply, and thus did not assess or collect information about the facility's ability to meet the provision. *Standards for Internal Control in the Federal Government* states that management should ensure there are adequate means of obtaining information from external stakeholders, such as contracted inspectors, that may have a significant impact on the agency achieving its goals.[77] Given that ERO performs the majority of SAAPI inspections under the 2008 PBNDS—27 of 29 in fiscal year 2013—incomplete assessment of these provisions can result in ERO having incomplete information about the extent to which facilities are prepared to maintain sexual abuse and assault allegation records, should such incidents occur. Developing a process to monitor the results of ERO inspections conducted under the 2008 SAAPI standard to ensure consistency across and completeness in how the inspections are performed, and addressing any inconsistencies, could help ensure that ERO management has complete information about relative SAAPI compliance across facilities.

ODO Inspections

ODO identified some deficiencies in facility compliance with ICE's three sets of SAAPI standards during fiscal years 2010 through 2013.[78] In particular, ODO identified SAAPI deficiencies during 7 of 30 inspections (23 percent) at 28 facilities.[79] Similar to ERO inspection results, ODO inspection results identified deficiencies in priority provisions, such as the provision that staff be trained in required SAAPI areas (3 facilities). In addition, facilities did not meet SAAPI provisions to maintain separate general and investigative files for cases of sexual abuse or assault (2 facilities), specify that chain-of-command reporting sexual abuse and assault allegations includes reporting to ICE (1 facility), or use a coordinated, multidisciplinary team approach to respond to sexual abuse (1 facility). ODO officials stated that they have not identified any trends among facilities with deficient SAAPI provisions. Our review of corrective action plans showed that corrective actions were taken at 6 of 7 facilities,

---

[77]GAO/AIMD-00-21.3.1.

[78]Our analysis included inspection reports available as of August 13, 2013. At that time, all but 3 inspection reports scheduled for fiscal year 2013 were available for our review. ODO inspectors do not use the inspection checklist ERO inspectors use or assess if a facility has overall met or not met a standard. Instead, ODO inspectors review the conditions at a facility against the SAAPI standard text to identify deficiencies. As a result, we did not quantify unmet components of the SAAPI standard found by ODO inspections.

[79]ODO performed 4 of these inspections under the 2008 PBNDS, 2 under the 2007 Family Residential Standards, and 1 under the 2011 PBNDS.

DSMs and Self-assessments	and that another facility had received an extension from ICE to do so as of September 2013.

ERO officials provided an example of one deficiency in facility compliance with ICE's three sets of SAAPI provisions identified through DSM oversight, and ERO officials said their review of facility self-assessment results identified deficiencies in the SAAPI provisions at more than a third of facilities. In regard to the DSM program, ERO officials said they received weekly reports from DSMs who performed on-site oversight at approximately 50 facilities during fiscal years 2010 through 2013. ERO officials provided one example of a SAAPI-related deficiency identified through a DSM weekly report.[80] In this instance, a DSM determined that a facility was not in compliance with staff training requirements, including SAAPI-related requirements. In regard to the self-assessment program, ERO officials reported in September 2013 that they reviewed inspection results from the 93 facilities, which collectively housed less than 1 percent of ICE's detainee population during fiscal years 2010 through 2012, and that the inspection results identified deficiencies in compliance with at least one SAAPI provision or with the overall SAAPI standard at 39 facilities. The self-assessment program policy guidelines require that facilities include corrective action plans for any deficiencies that the facility did not correct at the time of the assessment in their results. According to ERO officials, the 39 facilities included corrective actions to address the SAAPI deficiencies they identified in their assessments, and as of September 2013, had completed or were in the process of implementing the actions.[81]

---

[80]We did not independently review DSM weekly reports to determine the frequency with which DSMs identified SAAPI-related deficiencies.

[81]We did not review the self-assessment inspection results or corrective actions because ERO was in the process of collecting facility self-assessment results for the first year of the self-assessment program during our audit work.

GAO-14-38 Immigration Detention

USMS Inspections	In August 2013, DOJ-certified auditors were to conduct audits of facilities subject to the DOJ PREA rule, including the 125 facilities that are under agreement with USMS and house ICE detainees.[82] In particular, DOJ's PREA rule requires that the agencies managing these facilities ensure that the facilities undergo triennial PREA audits, and that agencies publish final PREA audit reports on their websites, or make these reports otherwise publicly available.[83] Following finalization of DOJ's PREA rule, USMS added a question to its annual inspection checklist concerning the extent to which the facility is compliant with all applicable PREA standards. USMS officials responsible for prisoner operations explained that they plan to use results of these triennial PREA audit reports to determine facility compliance with PREA per the USMS annual inspection checklist.[84] ERO officials responsible for detention oversight stated that as the DOJ PREA audits are fairly recent, they have not yet determined to what extent, if any, they will use the DOJ audit results to inform ICE's oversight of SAAPI provisions at USMS facilities that house ICE detainees.

[82]In addition to oversight performed by ICE and DOJ, the American Correctional Association is also to monitor select ICE facilities according to its own SAAPI detention standards for the purpose of providing facility accreditation. ICE officials stated that while the ICE detention standards were based on American Correctional Association standards, ICE does not request American Correctional Association inspection results because, as American Correctional Association officials told us, these results are considered proprietary. ICE officials further stated that ICE recognizes value in facilities maintaining American Correctional Association and other accreditations, but ICE standards are tailored to meet the unique needs of its immigrant population, and ICE relies on its own standards as the best measure of whether facilities are providing appropriate conditions of confinement. ERO performed SAAPI oversight at about half of these facilities (68 of 125) through inspections, self-assessments, or on-site monitoring through the DSM program. According to ERO officials, the remaining 57 facilities are inspected under the NDS, which do not include SAAPI provisions.

[83]28 C.F.R. §§ 115.401(a), 115.403(f). The DOJ PREA rule defines an agency as the unit of a state, local, corporate, or nonprofit authority, or of DOJ, with direct responsibility for the operation of any facility that confines inmates, detainees, or residents, including the implementation of policy as set by the governing, corporate, or nonprofit authority. See 28 C.F.R. § 115.5.

[84]Prior to October 2012, USMS did not collect SAAPI-related information through its inspection process.

ICE Plans to Increase On-site Monitoring at Select Facilities and Self-assessments at Others

ERO plans to increase oversight at some facilities and the use of self-assessments at other facilities, based on relative average daily detainee populations and success in past inspections, with an attendant benefit of potentially achieving cost savings for detention management. Moving forward, ERO officials said they plan to expand use of DSMs to an additional 22 facilities, targeting those facilities that house a relatively large proportion of ICE detainees.[85] ERO officials responsible for the DSM program stated that DSMs directly contribute to ICE cost savings because, by better ensuring facility compliance with detention standards, they prevent ICE from potentially incurring future costs.[86] According to ERO officials, in January 2013, ICE planned to increase its use of self-assessments at other facilities that have relatively low average daily populations, house detainees for more than 72 hours, and that passed ICE inspections in the past 2 years.[87] ERO will assess compliance at these facilities biennially instead of annually, and these facilities will be required to complete self-assessments the year that ERO does not inspect them. For example, ERO officials stated that facilities eligible for biennial inspections in January 2013 will then complete a self-assessment in 2014. As of August 2013, in addition to the 93 facilities that completed annual self-assessments, ICE approved 36 facilities for biennial inspections. According to ERO officials responsible for oversight, ICE largely discontinued annual inspections at facilities that house detainees for less than 72 hours and implemented biennial inspections at other facilities in an effort to lower detention costs. In addition, officials explained that using self-assessments as an oversight mechanism is considered low risk because these facilities house detainees for a relatively short period of time.

---

[85]As of August 2013, ERO officials said they have not decided in which facilities ERO will place these 22 DSMs, and thus could not determine how the additional DSMs would increase the average detainee daily population monitored by DSMs.

[86]ERO officials responsible for the DSM program explained that these cost savings could be related to detention areas other than SAAPI. For example, a DSM that ensures a facility's medical unit examines sick detainees on a timely basis could curtail future detainee health care costs. In addition, these officials stated that it would be difficult to estimate the extent to which DSM oversight has contributed to ICE cost savings because it is challenging to quantify the future costs DSMs have saved through their preventive actions.

[87]Specifically, facilities selected for biennial inspections must house an average daily population of greater than10 detainees but fewer than 50 detainees for more than 72 hours.

Further changes to DHS oversight of SAAPI compliance at detention facilities may occur in the course of implementing DHS's final PREA rule. For example, the DHS PREA notice of proposed rulemaking would provide for facility audits on a triennial cycle, in addition to ICE's current annual and biennial inspection schedule.[88] In addition, the notice of proposed rulemaking would require that ICE publish final inspection reports on its website, or make them otherwise readily available to the public.

Conclusions

ICE has taken action to strengthen sexual abuse and assault prevention and intervention at its detention facilities; however, some improvements could further strengthen ICE management of its detention program in this regard. For example, to assess and ensure the safety and security of detainees, it is important that ICE detention management programs have complete and accurate information with which to assess program results and take corrective action, as necessary. By developing and implementing additional internal controls to ensure reporting of sexual abuse and assault allegations by ERO field offices, ICE could better ensure the completeness of JICMS sexual abuse data and thereby strengthen these data's usefulness for making detention management decisions and meeting program management goals. In addition, by clarifying guidance to help ensure that ICE and facility administrators correctly document investigations into sexual abuse and assault allegations, ICE could better ensure the completeness of facility files for SAAPI program management purposes and better position ICE and facility administrators to comply with the provisions of the DHS notice of proposed rulemaking. ICE also has opportunities to better ensure the quality of information available to its managers for SAAPI program planning and improve its oversight of existing SAAPI provisions. In particular, by documenting and maintaining reliable information on the detention standards cited in facilities' contracts and agreements, as well as recording any agreements by facilities to undergo inspection under more rigorous standards, ICE could better ensure that ICE officials, facility administrators, and other stakeholders have a reliable and consistent understanding of facility detention standards and plan for the resources and time necessary to implement DHS's PREA notice of

---

[88]DHS may expedite inspection in the event that it believes that a particular facility may be experiencing sexual abuse and assault problems.

proposed rulemaking. In addition, developing a process to monitor the results of ERO inspections conducted under the 2008 SAAPI standard to ensure consistency across and completeness in how the inspections are performed, and addressing any inconsistencies, could help ensure that ERO management has complete information about relative and actual SAAPI compliance across facilities. Further, OIG and ERO coordination to ensure that the OIG has access to OIG hotline connectivity data, could better ensure that the OIG has information it needs to identify and address any technical issues detainees face in trying to reaching the hotline.

Recommendations for Executive Action

To ensure that ICE has complete and accurate information needed for SAAPI program decision making and planning, we recommend that the Director of ICE take the following four actions:

- develop and implement additional internal controls to ensure ERO field offices' reporting of allegations of sexual abuse and assault to the Joint Intake Center;
- clarify guidance for ICE and facility administrators on how to correctly document investigations into sexual abuse and assault allegations;
- document and maintain reliable information on the detention standards cited in facilities' contracts and agreements, and record any agreements by facilities to undergo inspection under more rigorous standards; and
- develop a process to monitor the results of ERO annual inspections conducted under the 2008 SAAPI standard to ensure consistency across the inspections and completeness in how the inspections are performed, and address any inconsistencies.

In addition, to ensure that the DHS OIG has information for identifying and addressing any technical problems detainees face in reaching the OIG hotline, we recommend that the Director of ICE and the DHS Deputy Inspector General coordinate OIG access to OIG hotline connectivity data.

Agency Comments and Our Evaluation

We provided a draft of this report to DHS and DOJ for their review and comment. DHS provided written comments, which are reproduced in appendix VIII, and DOJ did not provide written comments. In its comments, DHS concurred with the five recommendations and described actions under way or planned to address them by April 30, 2014. DHS and DOJ provided technical comments, which we incorporated as appropriate.

With regard to the first recommendation, that ICE develop and implement additional internal controls to ensure field offices' reporting of sexual abuse and assault allegations to the Joint Intake Center, DHS concurred and stated that ICE has taken action, and plans to take additional action, to better ensure ERO field offices' reporting of such allegations. Specifically, DHS stated that ICE issued a directive and developed guidance and training materials to enhance field office reporting of sexual abuse and assault allegations, as discussed in our report, and would take further steps to issue supplemental guidance. Further, DHS noted that ODO compares system data with field office records during visits, which it completes at a sample of facilities, to assess compliance with reporting requirements, and stated that future ICE quarterly reports to agency leadership will include any identified reporting discrepancies. These actions to educate and train staff and inform agency leadership of compliance with reporting requirements are positive steps, but to be fully responsive to the intent of our recommendation, we encourage DHS to develop and implement additional controls to assess compliance with reporting requirements across detention facilities, such as additional controls to help better ensure that ERO field office officials are reporting sexual abuse and assault allegations in accordance with ICE's directive. In addition, DHS noted that ERO field office officials at facilities we visited had reported two of the three allegations we reported as missing from ICE headquarters' information system; however, in its technical comments, DHS clarified that officials did not report these two allegations in accordance with protocols established in ICE's directive. We updated our final report to include this information.

With regard to the second recommendation, that ICE clarify guidance on how to correctly document investigations into sexual abuse and assault allegations, DHS concurred and noted the importance of completely documenting investigations of sexual abuse and assault allegations and described actions that ICE has taken and plans to take to clarify these requirements. Specifically, DHS stated that ICE plans to issue a broadcast message to all field offices providing detailed guidance to be disseminated and posted in all facilities. The department also noted that the facility files we reviewed included files for cases that originated in fiscal years 2010 through 2012, and that the number of facilities that have adopted detention standards that articulate specific requirements for facilities to maintain investigative files for sexual abuse allegations—the 2007 Residential Standards, 2008 PBNDS, and 2011 PBNDS—have increased since that time. However, as described in the report, while additional facilities may have moved to adopt these detention standards, four of the eight facilities at which we identified deficiencies in the investigative files were already governed by these standards at the time the allegations associated with the files were made. Accordingly, if fully implemented, ICE's planned action to distribute detailed guidance should help address the intent of the recommendation to better ensure the completeness of facility investigative files.

With regard to the third recommendation, that ICE document and maintain reliable information on the detention standards cited in facilities' contracts and agreements, DHS concurred and cited action it was taking to document and maintain reliable information, and record any agreements by facilities to undergo inspection under more rigorous standards. While DHS noted that deficiencies in record keeping did not affect ICE's efforts to safeguard detainees, DHS stated that it recognized the importance of thorough record keeping and that it is in the process of modifying its Facility Performance Management System to report data on both the standards that contractually govern a facility and the standards that a facility has voluntarily agreed to adopt for inspection purposes, and that ERO and OAQ will jointly review this list on a quarterly basis to ensure information on both categories is current and accurate. If fully implemented, these actions should address the intent of the recommendation and better position ICE headquarters officials, ERO field office officials, facility administrators, and other stakeholders to have a reliable and consistent understanding of applicable facility detention standards.

With regard to the fourth recommendation, that ICE develop a process to monitor the results of ERO annual inspections conducted under the 2008 SAAPI standard, DHS concurred and stated that the department will make every effort to ensure utilization of a uniform inspections protocol, including action to clarify expectations with inspectors and conduct monthly meetings with the inspection contractor to reinforce expectations. To assess the extent to which the contractor meets these expectations and to meet the intent of the recommendation, we encourage departmental efforts to develop a process to monitor the results of facility inspections and address any inconsistencies in how inspections are performed.

With regard to the fifth recommendation, that ICE and the DHS OIG coordinate access to hotline connectively data, DHS concurred and stated that the Director of ICE would immediately begin to provide the DHS Deputy Inspector General with information on OIG hotline connectivity exceptions, as appropriate. If implemented as planned, this action should help address the intent of the recommendation to ensure that the DHS OIG has information for identifying and addressing any technical problems detainees face in reporting sexual abuse allegations.

We are sending copies of this report to the appropriate congressional committees, the Acting Secretary of Homeland Security, the Attorney General of the United States, and other interested parties. In addition, the report is available at no charge on the GAO website at http://www.gao.gov.

If you or your staff have any questions, please contact me at (202) 512-8777 or gamblerr@gao.gov. Contact points for our Offices of Congressional Relations and Public Affairs may be found on the last page of this report. GAO staff who made significant contributions to this report are listed in appendix IX.

Rebecca Gambler
Director
Homeland Security and Justice

List of Requesters

The Honorable Zoe Lofgren
Ranking Member
Subcommittee on Immigration and Border Security
Committee on the Judiciary
House of Representatives

The Honorable Robert Brady
The Honorable Judy Chu
The Honorable Yvette Clarke
The Honorable Luis V. Gutierrez
The Honorable Janice Hahn
The Honorable Alcee Hastings
The Honorable Michael Honda
The Honorable Barbara Lee
The Honorable John Lewis
The Honorable Carolyn Maloney
The Honorable George Miller
The Honorable Gwen Moore
The Honorable James Moran
The Honorable Eleanor Holmes Norton
The Honorable Jared Polis
The Honorable Mike Quigley
The Honorable Charles Rangel
The Honorable Lucille Roybal-Allard
The Honorable Loretta Sanchez
The Honorable Jose Serrano
The Honorable Nydia Velazquez
The Honorable Henry Waxman
House of Representatives

Appendix I: Objectives, Scope, and Methodology

This report addresses the following three questions:

(1) What do Department of Homeland Security (DHS) data show about sexual abuse and assault in immigration detention facilities, and how are these data used for detention management?

(2) To what extent has DHS included provisions for addressing sexual abuse and assault in its immigration detention standards?

(3) To what extent has DHS assessed facility administrator compliance with these provisions and what were the results of DHS's assessments?

For this report, we assessed DHS's efforts to mitigate sexual abuse and assault in immigration detention facilities that house U.S. Immigration and Customs Enforcement (ICE) detainees. DHS defines an immigration detention facility as a confinement facility operated by or affiliated with ICE that routinely holds persons for over 24 hours. We did not include other types of facilities, such as holding facilities and prisons that temporarily house detainees waiting for ICE transfer to detention facilities. We also excluded the three federal prisons where ICE has detention bed space because two house few detainees and use of the third prison for detention was to be discontinued by the end of calendar year 2013, according to Bureau of Prisons and ICE officials. We also did not include facilities for juveniles that are regulated by the Department of Health and Human Services.

To address our questions, we visited a nonprobability sample of 10 detention facilities in California, Florida, Texas, and Washington. We selected these facilities based on a mix of factors, such as differences in geographical location, detainee population, facility type, detention standards governing the facility, length of time the facility may hold detainees, and recommendations made by DHS and organizations that work with immigration detainees.[1] We collected and reviewed investigative files for all 70 sexual abuse and assault allegations occurring from fiscal years 2010 through fiscal year 2012 maintained at the 10 facilities we visited and assessed their completeness and the extent to which they are useful for detention management against ICE

---

[1]We did not use the number of sexual abuse allegations at a facility as part of our selection criteria because a high number of allegations could represent either (1) an increased risk of abuse to detainees or (2) increased reporting at a facility.

requirements and *Standards for Internal Control in the Federal Government*.[2] Of these files, we selected investigative files for a nonprobability sample of 15 allegations for more in-depth analysis, to include allegations from each facility and allegations against staff members and allegations against detainees. The results of our more in-depth analysis are not generalizable to all investigative files, but provided helpful insights into investigative file completeness. We interviewed ICE Enforcement and Removal Operations (ERO) field office officials, ERO detention service managers (DSM), facility administrators, and medical personnel regarding sexual abuse and assault prevention and intervention (SAAPI) policies and procedures in place at the facility. We also interviewed 18 guards at 9 of these facilities to understand how these policies and procedures are practiced.[3] Moreover, we interviewed a nonprobability sample of 53 detainees to gain an understanding of detainees' knowledge of policies relevant to SAAPI, such as how to report sexual abuse or assault. We selected approximately 6 detainees from each of the 9 facilities.[4] We selected detainees based on gender, age, country of origin, and number of days in ICE custody. Detainees speak various languages, and some detainees are not proficient in English. Toward including such detainees in our sample, we interviewed 19 detainees at 5 facilities in Spanish, but did not interview detainees who were not proficient in English or Spanish. In addition, we conducted physical observations to observe facility implementation of SAAPI provisions, such as posting required information. The information we obtained from our facility visits cannot be generalized to all facilities, guards, or detainees but offers insight into the overall range of SAAPI implementation across detention facilities. In advance of each site visit, we interviewed a local immigrant advocacy organization to gain its perspective on ICE's efforts to prevent and respond to sexual abuse and assault at the facility and the extent to which sexual abuse and assault in detention may be over- or underreported and why. We identified these local organizations through recommendations provided by two national advocacy organizations—the American Civil Liberties Union and the

---

[2]GAO/AIMD-00-21.3.1.

[3]When possible, we selected the guards to include one female and one male guard at each facility. Guards at one facility elected not to speak with us at the recommendation of their union, which was concerned that information guards shared with us could be used by facility management to negatively assess guard performance.

[4]The 10th facility did not have any detainees in its custody during our visit.

National Immigrant Justice Center. In instances when the national
organizations suggested that we speak with more than one local
organization, we invited representatives from all of the local organizations
to meet with us. While not generalizable, this sample of organizations
provided us with helpful insights into the perspectives of local advocacy
organizations.

To determine what DHS data show about sexual abuse and assault in
detention facilities and how they are used for detention management, we
reviewed closing reports summarizing the allegation and investigative
steps and outcomes for all 215 sexual abuse and assault allegations
reported to ICE from October 2009 through March 2013 and tracked in
ICE Office of Professional Responsibility's (OPR) Joint Integrity Case
Management System (JICMS)—the primary system ICE uses to track
sexual assault and abuse allegations.[5] We analyzed this information to
determine the characteristics of these allegations and how they were
reported. We also met with agency officials from ICE offices and other
DHS components with responsibilities related to collecting and using data
on sexual abuse and assault in detention facilities including (1) ICE OPR,
which tracks and investigates sexual abuse allegations; (2) ICE Office of
Detention Policy and Planning (ODPP), which develops policies and
standards to address sexual abuse in detention facilities; (3) the DHS
Office of Inspector General (OIG), which investigates misconduct
involving DHS and contractor employees and operates a hotline through
which detainees can report complaints regarding misconduct in detention
facilities, including sexual abuse and assault; and (4) the DHS Office for
Civil Rights and Civil Liberties, which is responsible for identifying policy
gaps that can contribute to sexual abuse. To assess the reliability of the
JICMS data, we compared the allegations contained in JICMS, which
according to ICE officials, is to include all reported sexual abuse and
assault allegations, with information from other sources, including
allegations documented by the 10 facilities we visited. Further, we
interviewed knowledgeable OPR officials about the completeness and
reliability of JICMS data and controls in place for these data, and

---

[5]We selected October 2009 because, according to ICE officials, data prior to fiscal year
2010 do not include sexual abuse and assault allegations against detainees. According to
ICE OPR, it did not collect this information in JICMS prior to fiscal year 2010 because the
office was focused on employee and contractor misconduct, in accordance with its
mission. We selected March 2013 because OPR had completed most investigations into
allegations made through then at the time of our review.

assessed our findings against ICE requirements and *Standards for
Internal Control in the Federal Government.*[6] We determined that the data
within JICMS were sufficiently reliable for the purpose of presenting the
type and outcome of sexual abuse and assault allegations in JICMS, but
we found limitations with the information about the number of reported
sexual abuse allegations, which we discuss in the report. To assess
barriers to detainees reporting sexual abuse, we interviewed
knowledgeable ICE officials regarding the extent to which sexual abuse
may be over- or underreported, and reviewed relevant documentation
from the Department of Justice's (DOJ) Bureau of Justice Statistics. We
also conducted limited testing of reporting mechanisms at each of the
facilities we visited by placing calls to ICE hotlines from 19 telephones in
detainee housing areas at 10 facilities, among other things. We generally
tested a telephone in two living area pods at each facility we visited by
dialing the OIG hotline, ICE Community and Detainee Helpline, and the
ICE Joint Intake Center hotline. In addition, we collected and analyzed
telephone connectivity data from ERO to determine the extent to which
detainee calls placed to the OIG hotline from fiscal years 2010 through
2012 using ICE's telephone contractor or its pro bono telephone platform
were successfully connected.[7] We also interviewed ERO and OIG
officials about how they use these data and assessed our findings against
Standards for Internal Control in the Federal Government.[8] We assessed
the reliability of these data by interviewing ERO officials and contractor
personnel familiar with the processes used to collect, record, and analyze
the data, and determined that the data were sufficiently reliable for the
purposes of our report. We identified and analyzed DHS and ICE policies
related to sexual abuse and assault reporting requirements and plans for
using sexual abuse data for detention management. Finally, we assessed
the completeness of documentation in 15 sexual abuse and assault
investigative files maintained at the 10 facilities we visited against ICE

---

[6]GAO/AIMD-00-21.3.1.

[7]ERO officials explained that ICE contracts with one telephone company to provide full
telephone service for detainees at 18 of its 251 detention facilities. In addition, about 191
ICE intergovernmental service agreement facilities use this telephone company's
nationwide pro bono platform, which enables detainees to place calls at no charge to
certain numbers, including the OIG hotline, among others.

[8]GAO/AIMD-00-21.3.1.

requirements and *Standards for Internal Control in the Federal Government.*[9]

To determine the extent to which DHS detention standards include SAAPI provisions, we reviewed sexual abuse and assault standards and policies developed by ICE's ODPP, Office of the Principal Legal Advisor, and ICE Health Service Corps currently applicable to, or proposed for, ICE detention facilities. In particular, to establish the relative protections these standards afford detainees, we compared the

- 2000 National Detention Standards (NDS),
- 2007 Family Residential Standards,
- 2008 Performance-Based National Detention Standards (PBNDS),
- 2011 PBNDS, and
- DHS's notice of proposed rulemaking on the Prison Rape and Elimination Act (PREA).[10]

Moreover, we compared DHS's 2011 PBNDS and PREA notice of proposed rulemaking with recommendations for immigration detention centers that the National Prison Rape Elimination Commission (NPREC) made in 2009, and interviewed seven of eight former NPREC members to obtain their perspectives on how the extent to which DHS incorporated NPREC's recommendations will affect the effectiveness of DHS's SAAPI efforts.[11] We also interviewed DHS Office of the Principal Legal Advisor and ODPP officials about the department's reasons for incorporating or not incorporating particular NPREC recommendations in the 2011 PBNDS.[12] In addition, we interviewed representatives from national organizations and associations involved in immigration detention advocacy to obtain their perspectives on DHS's PREA notice of proposed rulemaking. In particular, we spoke with the American Civil Liberties Union, American Bar Association, National Immigrant Justice Center, and

---

[9]GAO/AIMD-00-21.3.1.

[10]Standards to Prevent, Detect, and Respond to Sexual Abuse and Assault in Confinement Facilities, 77 Fed. Reg. 75,300 (Dec. 19, 2012).

[11]The other commissioner was not available for comment.

[12]We did not interview DHS officials about the reasons for incorporating or not incorporating particular NPREC recommendations in DHS's proposed PREA rule because it is in proposed form and subject to change based on public comments received by the department.

Just Detention International. We selected these organizations and associations based on their involvement with SAAPI-related immigration detention issues and contributions to the development of national detention standards. While not generalizable, this sample provided us with helpful insights into the perspectives of national advocacy organizations. In addition, we compared DHS's PREA notice of proposed rulemaking and DOJ's final PREA rule to determine differences, if any, in sexual abuse and assault provisions they include. To determine which sexual abuse and assault standards ICE requires facilities to implement, we requested fiscal year 2013 information from ERO and the ICE Office of Acquisition Management (OAQ) concerning the detention standards cited in facilities' contracts or agreements with ICE. We assessed the reliability of the ERO and OAQ detention standards data by reviewing the contracts and agreements on which the information was based for a nonprobability sample of 20 facilities, and interviewing ERO and OAQ officials about discrepancies in the data.[13] We assessed ERO's and OAQ's maintenance of information on the standards cited in facilities' contracts and agreements against *Standards for Internal Control in the Federal Government*.[14] We determined that the data were sufficiently reliable for the purpose of presenting trends in the standards to which different types of facilities are to adhere, but we found limitations with the data the detention standards cited in facilities' contracts and agreements, which we discuss in the report. Finally, we interviewed relevant DHS officials regarding their approach to implementing the 2011 PBNDS and PREA notice of proposed rulemaking across facilities and any associated challenges.

To determine the extent to which DHS assessed facility compliance with SAAPI provisions, as well as the results of these assessments, we reviewed oversight mechanisms utilized at ICE's detention facilities from fiscal years 2010 through 2013. In particular, we compared oversight mechanisms in place through (1) ERO annual facility inspections, (2) ERO's DSM program, (3) ERO's Operational Review Self-Assessment process, and (4) OPR Office of Detention Oversight's (ODO) risk-based

---

[13]We selected this sample to include (1) facilities at which we conducted site visits and (2) facilities for which ERO and OAQ information on facility standards differed. While not generalizable, this sample provided us with helpful insights into the reliability of ERO and OAQ's information on facility standards.

[14]GAO/AIMD-00-21.3.1.

facility inspections and assessed the extent to which these mechanisms
where used at ICE's 251 authorized facilities. In addition, we reviewed the
results of the 110 ERO and 30 ODO facility inspection reports that
assessed compliance with SAAPI standards during fiscal years 2010
through 2013.[15] We analyzed information in these reports to assess the
extent to which inspectors found deficiencies in the SAAPI standards,
associated corrective actions, and any patterns across reports. In
addition, we assessed the consistency of the SAAPI inspections with
standards in *Standards for Internal Control in the Federal Government*.[16]
We also interviewed ERO and ODO officials responsible for inspections
and the DSM program; officials from the entity that ERO currently
contracts with to complete its inspections; DSMs, ICE officials, and
administrators responsible for on-site oversight at the facilities we visited;
ERO officials responsible for reviewing results from facility self-
assessments; and U.S. Marshals Service (USMS) officials responsible for
assessing compliance with DOJ standards at the facilities with which
USMS has agreements that house ICE detainees about the oversight
they perform.[17] Moreover, we collected information on ICE's plans for
future oversight and DHS's notice of proposed rulemaking to assess the
extent to which they will change ICE's SAAPI oversight efforts.

We conducted this performance audit from October 2012 through
November 2013, in accordance with generally accepted government
auditing standards. Those standards require that we plan and perform the
audit to obtain sufficient, appropriate evidence to provide a reasonable
basis for our findings and conclusions based on our audit objectives. We
believe that the evidence obtained provides a reasonable basis for our
findings and conclusions based on our audit objectives.

---

[15]We chose this time frame because prior to fiscal year 2010, the scope of ICE's
inspections of the SAAPI standard was limited to 2 of its 251 facilities. Because the 2000
NDS do not include a SAAPI standard, we reviewed reports inspecting the 2007
Residential Standards, 2008 PBNDS, or 2011 PBNDS. In addition, our analysis included
inspection reports available as of August 2013. At that time, all but 2 ERO and 3 ODO
inspection reports scheduled for fiscal year 2013 were available for our review.

[16]GAO/AIMD-00-21.3.1.

[17]From fiscal years 2011 through 2013, ERO contracted with the Nakamoto Group to
conduct its annual detention standards inspections.

Appendix II: Summary of Substantiated Sexual Abuse and Assault Allegations, October 2009 through March 2013

Our analysis of ICE JICMS data showed 15 substantiated allegations of sexual abuse and assault in ICE detention facilities from October 2009 through March 2013. The 15 substantiated sexual abuse and assault cases had several similar underlying factors. In particular, 4 of these cases included situations where the detainee was alone with a guard—such as in protective custody or transport—and 3 cases involved transgender victims. In addition, 4 cases included a perpetrator who did not understand the zero-tolerance sexual abuse policy. In 4 of the 15 substantiated cases, a guard sexually abused a detainee, whereas in the remaining 11 cases, a detainee sexually abused a detainee. Table 10 summarizes these substantiated allegations and identifies characteristics that were similar across multiple cases.

Table 10: Substantiated Allegations of Sexual Abuse and Assault in U.S. Immigration and Customs Enforcement (ICE) Detention Facilities, October 2009 through March 2013

Allegation summary[a]	Type of facility	Outcomes	Similarities across cases
Staff-on-detainee allegations			
A transgender detainee was sexually assaulted by a male guard while in protective housing (December 2010).	Dedicated intergovernmental service agreement	The guard was prosecuted by the local U.S. Attorney's Office (USAO).	• Transgender victim. • Victim housed in protective custody. • Staff member alone with detainee. • Perpetrator admitted to abuse.
A female guard attempted sexual intercourse with a male detainee (November 2012).	Service processing center	Criminal prosecution was declined by the local USAO.	• Staff member alone with detainee. • Perpetrator admitted to abuse.
A male guard took a female detainee out of the vehicle during transport to an airport, conducted a pat-down search, and asked her to raise her shirt. When the detainee refused, the guard propositioned her for sexual intercourse. The detainee refused and they proceeded to the airport. During an investigation, an additional nine female detainees reported that this male guard had sexually assaulted them during transport (December 2009 to May 2010).	Dedicated intergovernmental service agreement	The guard was prosecuted and indicted by the local USAO.	• Staff member alone with detainee. • Perpetrator admitted to abuse.

Allegation summary[a]	Type of facility	Outcomes	Similarities across cases
A male guard intimidated and coerced a transgender male detainee assigned to protective custody to display his breasts and then the guard inappropriately touched himself in view of the detainee (December 2009).	Nondedicated intergovernmental service agreement	The guard was prosecuted in state court.	• Transgender victim. • Victim housed in protective custody. • Staff member alone with detainee. • Perpetrator admitted to abuse.
Detainee-on-detainee allegations			
A male detainee was sexually assaulted by another male detainee. The assault included repeated sexual requests, among other things (February to March 2010).	Nondedicated intergovernmental service agreement	The local law enforcement agency did not pursue an investigation because the alleged perpetrator was scheduled for deportation 1 week after the allegation.	• Victim housed in protective custody.
A male detainee repeatedly hit another male detainee in the face with his genitalia (September 2010).	Nondedicated intergovernmental service agreement	The perpetrator was tried for sexual misconduct and ordered to pay a fine.	• Transgender victim.
A male detainee touched another male detainee's genitalia on several occasions (March 2013).	Nondedicated intergovernmental service agreement	The local district attorney did not pursue prosecution because the victim did not want to press charges.	• Perpetrator did not understand zero-tolerance sexual abuse and assault policy. • Perpetrator admitted to abuse.
A male detainee grabbed two other males' buttocks (January 2013).	Contract detention facility	The local law enforcement agency did not file criminal charges.	• Perpetrator admitted to abuse.
A male detainee grabbed another male detainee by his genitalia (September 2011).	Contract detention facility	Criminal prosecution was declined by the local USAO.	• Perpetrator did not understand zero-tolerance sexual abuse and assault policy. • Perpetrator admitted to abuse.
A male detainee grabbed another male detainee's genitalia (March 2013).	Nondedicated intergovernmental service agreement	Local law enforcement declined to investigate because the victim did not want to press charges.	• None.

Allegation summary[a]	Type of facility	Outcomes	Similarities across cases
A male detainee reported that other male detainees touched him, and an investigation indicated that there was inappropriate touching among ICE detainees, but that there was no oral sex or penetration (November 2012).	Nondedicated intergovernmental service agreement	None of the individuals involved wanted to file or sign a formal complaint regarding the incident.	• Perpetrators admitted to abuse.
A male detainee pressed his genitalia against another male detainee (January 2013).	Nondedicated intergovernmental service agreement	The local district attorney declined prosecution because of a lack of evidence.	• Perpetrator admitted to abuse.
A male detainee grabbed another male detainee's chest and buttocks (February 2013).	Nondedicated intergovernmental service agreement	Local law enforcement declined to investigate because the victim did not want to press charges.	• Perpetrator admitted to abuse.
A female detainee grabbed another female detainee's buttocks (June 2012).	Nondedicated intergovernmental service agreement	Local law enforcement declined to investigate because of the minor level of contact.	• Perpetrator did not understand zero-tolerance sexual abuse and assault policy.
A male detainee repeatedly requested oral sex from another male detainee (February 2013).	Nondedicated intergovernmental service agreement	The perpetrator was transferred before a disciplinary hearing could take place.	• None.

Source: GAO analysis of ICE information.

[a]Dates presented in this column reflect when the alleged abuse occurred or, if that date was not available, when the allegation was reported to ICE headquarters.

Appendix III: Process for Reporting and Investigating Sexual Abuse and Assault Allegations

DHS ICE provides detainees with multiple methods to report sexual abuse and assault in detention facilities and oversees a multilayered investigation process. As shown in figure 3, detainees can report sexual abuse and assault allegations either locally at facilities in which they are housed or to DHS headquarters hotlines. Regardless of how detainees report abuse, DHS components are to forward these allegations to the Joint Intake Center to be routed for investigation. Local law enforcement and various DHS investigative entities including the OIG and ICE OPR conduct investigations into sexual abuse allegations. These investigations determine whether the alleged incident occurred and can lead to prosecution of alleged perpetrators.

Figure 3: Process for Reporting and Investigating Sexual Abuse Allegations in Immigration and Customs Enforcement (ICE) Detention Facilities

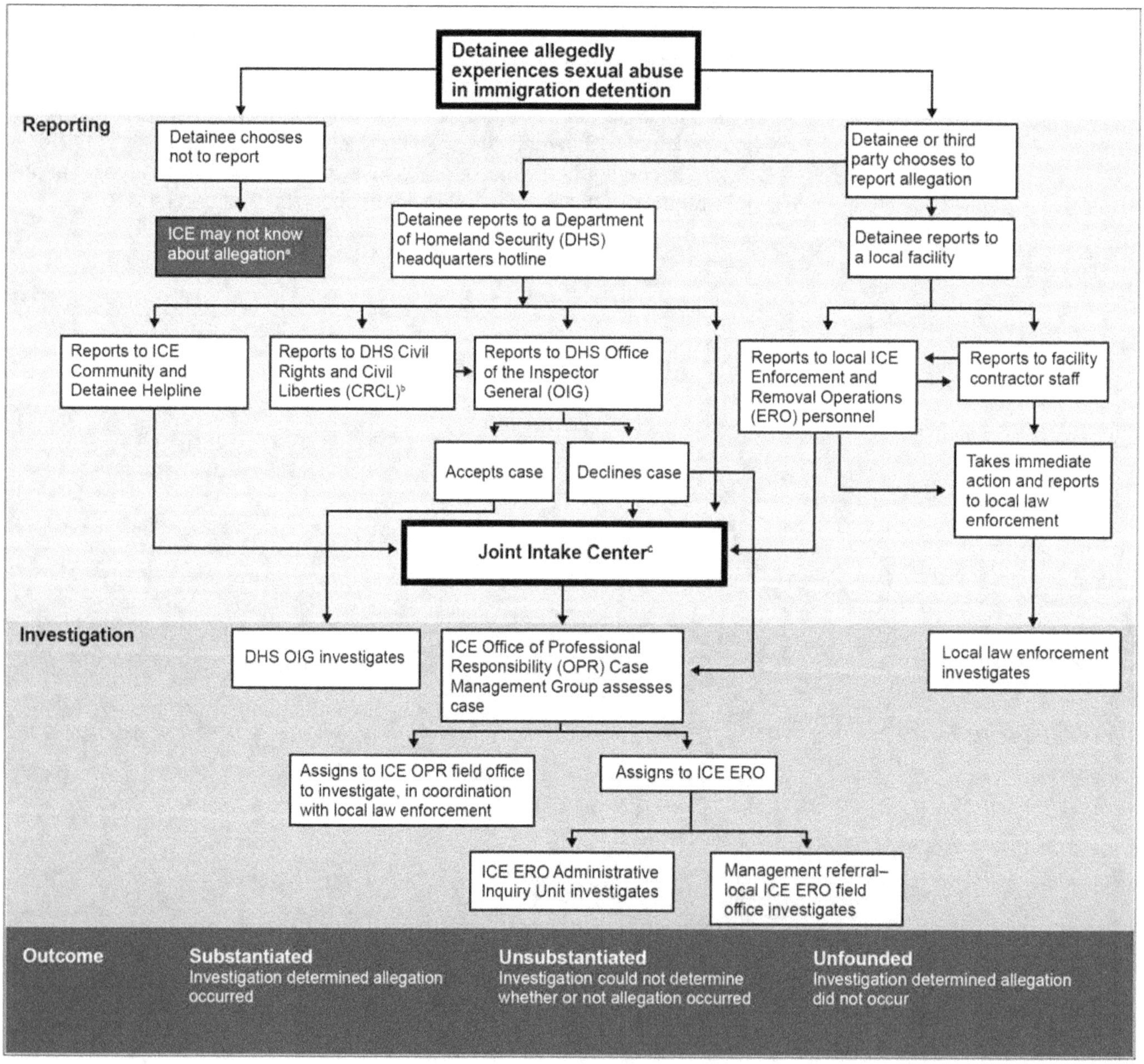

Source: GAO.

[a]According to ICE officials, facility staff receive training on signs of sexual abuse and assault and may be able to detect abuse even if a detainee or third party does not report it.

[b]According to Office for Civil Rights and Civil Liberties officials, the Office for Civil Rights and Civil Liberties first refers allegations it receives to the OIG. If the OIG declines to investigate the allegation, the Office for Civil Rights and Civil Liberties investigates the allegation or refers it to the ICE Prevention of Sexual Assault coordinator, who then refers it to the Joint Intake Center.

[c]When the Joint Intake Center receives staff-on-detainee allegations from ICE entities, it first refers them to the DHS OIG. If the DHS OIG declines to investigate the allegations, the Joint Intake Center refers them to OPR.

Appendix IV: Provisions for Sexual Abuse and Assault Prevention and Intervention Included in Immigration Detention Standards

Table 11 provides a summary comparing SAAPI provisions included in ICE'S detention standards that apply across immigration detention facilities. These standards include the 2000 NDS, 2008 PBNDS, and 2011 PBNDS.

Table 11: Provisions for Sexual Abuse and Assault Prevention and Intervention (SAAPI) in U.S. Immigration and Customs Enforcement (ICE) Detention Standards

Topical area	2000 National Detention Standards (NDS) provisions	2008 Performance-Based National Detention Standards (PBNDS) provisions	Provisions in 2011 PBNDS beyond those in 2008 PBNDS
Definitions	None related to SAAPI	Define detainee-on-detainee and staff-on-detainee sexual abuse or assault.	Expand definition of detainee-on-detainee sexual abuse or assault to include attempted sexually abusive contact. Expand definition of staff-on-detainee sexual abuse or assault to include repeated verbal statements or comments of a sexual nature to a detainee, including demeaning references to gender, derogatory comments about body or clothing, or profane or obscene language or gestures.
Prohibitions	Prohibit sexual assault, engaging in sexual acts, and making sexual proposals and threats	State that sexual conduct between detainees and staff, volunteers, or contract personnel—regardless of consensual status—is prohibited; and subject to administrative, disciplinary, and criminal sanctions.	Similar to the provisions in the 2008 SAAPI standard.
Written policies and procedures	None for SAAPI	Require facility administrators to have written SAAPI policies and procedures.	Require written SAAPI policies and procedures to include additional components, such as a statement of a zero-tolerance policy for all forms of sexual abuse or assault.
Program coordination	None for SAAPI	Require service processing centers and contract detention facilities to designate a SAAPI coordinator to, among other things, coordinate the gathering of reports on incidents of sexual abuse or assault.	Require all facilities that house detainees for more than 72 hours, including intergovernmental service agreement facilities, to designate a SAAPI coordinator.
Staff training	None specific to SAAPI	Require facilities to provide training on certain topics relating to sexual abuse and assault for employees, volunteers, and contract personnel.	Modify 2008 requirements to specify that the level and type of training for volunteers and contractors will be based on the services they provide and their level of contact with detainees, requires training on working with vulnerable populations, and requires facilities to maintain documentation to verify training.

Topical area	2000 National Detention Standards (NDS) provisions	2008 Performance-Based National Detention Standards (PBNDS) provisions	Provisions in 2011 PBNDS beyond those in 2008 PBNDS
Detainee notification, orientation, and instruction	None related to SAAPI	Require facilities to provide detainees with information on their SAAPI programs. Facility must provide detainees an option to report a sexual incident or situation to a designated staff member other than an immediate point-of-contact line officer and post sexual assault awareness information.	Require that facilities provide detainees with information on additional topics and document detainee participation in the instruction session, post the name of the SAAPI program coordinator or designated staff member and local organizations that can assist detainee victims, and take additional steps to strengthen language assistance for limited English proficient and illiterate detainees.
Prevention	None specific to SAAPI, but require facilities to prevent abuse through housing assignments that reduce low-threat detainees' exposure to danger	Assign staff and detainees responsibility for being alert for and reporting signs of potential situations in which sexual assault might occur. Facility must work to prevent abuse through detainee admission and housing assignments. In particular, detainees must be screened upon arrival for risk of sexual victimization or abusiveness, and monitored and counseled accordingly. Detainees considered likely to become victims must be placed in the least restrictive housing that is available and appropriate.	Specify that a detainee who is subjected to sexual abuse or assault shall not be returned to general population until proper reclassification, taking into consideration any increased vulnerability of the detainee as a result of the sexual abuse or assault, is completed.
Prompt and effective intervention	None specific to SAAPI, but require that facilities have a process for responding to detainee grievances	Require that staff take seriously all statements from detainees claiming to be victims of sexual assaults, offer alleged victims immediate protection from the assailant, refer the alleged victim for a medical examination, and follow all reporting requirements.	Require that facilities use a coordinated, multidisciplinary team approach to respond to sexual abuse that includes a medical practitioner, a mental health practitioner, a security staff member and an investigator from the assigned investigative entity, as well as representatives from outside entities that provide relevant services and expertise. Further require that care is taken to place the detainee in a supportive environment that represents the least restrictive housing option possible.
Reporting, notifications, and confidentiality	Require officers to document prohibited acts, which include sexual assault, that they witness or suspect	Emphasize importance of timely reporting of all sexual abuse and assault incidents and allegations, and outline specific reporting avenues for different types of assault incidents. Require confidentiality measures to limit information about the alleged victims to those who have a need to know.	Require that staff suspected of perpetrating abuse be removed from all duties requiring detainee contact pending the outcome of an investigation.

Topical area	2000 National Detention Standards (NDS) provisions	2008 Performance-Based National Detention Standards (PBNDS) provisions	Provisions in 2011 PBNDS beyond those in 2008 PBNDS
Investigation and prosecution	Require facilities to develop a process for investigating detainee grievances, including allegations, but do not specifically address sexual abuse or assault investigations	Stipulate that a sensitive and coordinated response is necessary when a detainee alleges sexual abuse or assault, and that all allegations are promptly and effectively investigated. Require that staff preserve the crime scene, when possible, and arrange for the victim to undergo a forensic medical examination, based on factors such as availability of in-house expertise and security considerations.	Require that all investigations into alleged sexual assault be prompt, thorough, objective, and conducted by trained investigators. In addition, the facility administrator must arrange for the victim to undergo an off-site forensic medical examination in all cases, rather than based on such factors as availability of in-house expertise and general security considerations. Also require the facility SAAPI coordinator to review the results of every investigation of sexual abuse to assess and improve prevention and response efforts.
Health care services and transfer of detainees to hospitals or other facilities	Require that facilities provide detainees with emergency medical care, but do not specifically address treatment for sexual abuse or assault victims	Require that victims of sexual assault must be referred to a community facility for treatment and gathering of evidence, when possible. If care is provided in-house, requires that health care professionals take particular steps (e.g., offer victims prophylactic treatment, as appropriate).	Specify that if a victim is treated by a community facility, prophylactic treatment, emergency contraception, and follow-up examinations for sexually transmitted diseases are be offered to victims, as appropriate.
Tracking	Require that investigative forms are completed according to facility policies, but do not include specific requirements for tracking sexual abuse or assault	Require facility administrators to maintain general and investigative files for allegations of sexual abuse that include information such as crime characteristics, a detailed reporting timeline, incident and investigative reports, medical forms, and supporting memos and videotapes.	Require that the SAAPI program coordinator undertake an annual review of aggregate data related to sexual abuse allegations and present the findings to the field office director and ICE Enforcement and Removal Operations (ERO) headquarters for use in determining changes to existing policies and practices to further the goal of eliminating sexual abuse.

Source: GAO analysis of ICE detention standards.

Note: ICE has developed another set of detention standards—the 2007 Family Residential Standards—for facilities that house families. As of August 2013, 1 of ICE's 251 detention facilities housed families, and this facility housed less than 1 percent of the average detainee population from fiscal years 2010 through 2012. The 2007 Family Residential Standards are not included in this table because this table focuses on facilities that generally house adult immigration detainees.

GAO-14-38 Immigration Detention

Appendix V: NPREC Recommendations Compared with DHS Detention Standards and PREA Notice of Proposed Rulemaking

The Prison Rape Elimination Act of 2003 established the National Prison Rape Elimination Commission to study the impacts of prison rape in the United States and charged NPREC with recommending standards for addressing prison rape for consideration in developing standards required by PREA.[1] In June 2009, NPREC issued a report with recommended standards, including specific recommendations for facilities that house immigration detainees.[2] According to DHS, the department took NPREC's recommendations for facilities that house immigration detainees into consideration along with input from other sources in its development of ICE's 2011 PBNDS. In addition, DHS stated in the PREA notice of proposed rulemaking that NPREC's recommendations for facilities that house immigration detainees are of particular interest to the department. Table 12 provides a summary of the NPREC recommended standards for immigration detention facilities compared with the standards in ICE's 2011 PBNDS and DHS's PREA notice of proposed rulemaking, along with perspectives we obtained from former NPREC members and ICE officials on reasons for, and the significance of, any differences.

---

[1]See 42 U.S.C. §§ 15606(a), (d)-(e), 15607(a)(1)-(2). PREA directed the Attorney General to adopt national standards for the detection, prevention, reduction, and punishment of prison rape and required that these standards be based on the independent judgment of the Attorney General, after giving due consideration to the NPREC recommended standards. In its final PREA rule, the Department of Justice determined that PREA encompasses any federal confinement facility, including immigration detention facilities, and that federal agencies, including DHS, would work with the Attorney General to issue rules or procedures that would satisfy the requirements of PREA, citing the section of PREA that required the Attorney General to give due consideration to NPREC's recommendations, 42 U.S.C. § 15607(a)(2). *See* 77 Fed. Reg. at 37113.

[2]National Prison Rape Elimination Commission, *National Prison Rape Elimination Commission Report*, June 2009.

Table 12: National Prison Rape Elimination Commission (NPREC) Recommended Standards for Immigration Detention Facilities Compared with Department of Homeland Security (DHS) 2011 Performance-Based National Detention Standards (PBNDS) and DHS Prison Rape Elimination Act of 2003 (PREA) Notice of Proposed Rulemaking (NPRM)

NPREC recommended standard	2011 PBNDS and DHS NPRM	Related comments by former NPREC Commissioners and U.S. Immigration and Customs Enforcement (ICE) officials[a]
Agreements with outside public entities and community service providers—The agency maintains copies of agreements, or documentation showing attempts to enter into agreements, with one or more local or national organizations that provide legal advocacy and confidential emotional support services for immigrant victims of crime.	Both require that facility administrators enter into or attempt to enter into agreements. Neither specifically requires that agencies maintain documentation showing that they entered or attempted to enter into agreements.	NPREC—An agency should maintain documentation as a matter of good business practice. Facilities should maintain this documentation as evidence to present to PREA auditors. ICE—Facility managers are compelled to maintain documentation of attempts to enter into agreements because while the 2011 PBNDS do not specifically require this documentation, inspectors are to review this documentation in conducting facility inspections.
Employee training and specialized training of investigators and medical and mental health care—Provides for special additional training to employees, including medical and mental health practitioners and investigators on the following topics: (1) cultural sensitivity toward diverse understandings of acceptable and unacceptable sexual behavior, (2) appropriate terms and concepts for discussing sex and sexual abuse with a culturally diverse population, (3) sensitivity and awareness regarding past trauma that may have been experienced by immigration detainees, and (4) knowledge of all existing resources for immigration detainees both inside and outside the facility that provide treatment and counseling for trauma and legal advocacy for victims.	The NPRM requires specialized staff training on coordination and health care issues, and on communicating effectively with detainees. The 2011 PBNDS also require training for staff on "cultural and language issues." Neither explicitly requires training focused on the four topics enumerated in the NPREC recommended standard.	NPREC—Emphasized importance for DHS to require training on the specific topics NPREC recommended because individuals with a background in corrections do not inherently possess this knowledge and detainees will not find facility efforts to prevent sexual abuse credible if sexual abuse and assault prevention and intervention (SAAPI) information is not provided in a manner that is respectful of their cultural norms. ICE—Agreed with NPREC standard; however, many of the state and local jails housing ICE detainees do not have the resources to provide this specialized training, especially given that most house very small populations of ICE detainees (to which such cultural issues would be applicable). ICE could explore the possibility of assisting facilities with this type of training in the future, depending on its own resources.
Inmate (detainee) education—Sexual abuse education for immigration detainees is provided at a time and in a manner that is separate from information provided about their immigration cases, in detainees' own languages and in terms that are culturally appropriate, and is conducted by a qualified individual with experience communicating about these issues with a diverse population.	Both require that facilities provide information to ICE detainees in a language or format that they understand. Neither explicitly requires that education be provided to detainees separately from information about their immigration cases, in terms that are culturally appropriate, or by a qualified individual with experience communicating about these issues with a diverse population.	NPREC—Incorporation of all elements is important. ICE—ICE policies require that facilities make SAAPI-related information available to detainees on an ongoing basis that provides detainees with the opportunity to learn about SAAPI issues separately from their immigration case. Reiterated that many of the state and local jails housing ICE detainees do not have the resources to provide specialized training to staff beyond the training already required by the PBNDS, but that ICE could explore the possibility of assisting facilities with this type of training in the future, depending on resources.

NPREC recommended standard	2011 PBNDS and DHS NPRM	Related comments by former NPREC Commissioners and U.S. Immigration and Customs Enforcement (ICE) officials[a]
Detainee Handbook—Every detainee is provided with an ICE *Detainee Handbook* upon admission to the facility, and a replacement is provided whenever a detainee's handbook is lost or damaged. The *Detainee Handbook* contains notice of the agency's zero-tolerance policy toward sexual abuse and contains all the agency's policies related to sexual abuse, including information about how to report an incident of sexual abuse and detainees' rights and responsibilities related to sexual abuse. The *Detainee Handbook* will inform immigration detainees how to contact organizations in the community that provide sexual abuse counseling and legal advocacy for detainee victims of sexual abuse. The *Detainee Handbook* will also inform detainees how to contact the DHS Office for Civil Rights and Civil Liberties, DHS Office of the Inspector General (OIG), and diplomatic or consular personnel.	Both require that the handbook be made available to all detainees, and that detainees be notified about the facility's zero-tolerance policy and how to report allegations of abuse to ICE headquarters and the OIG. Neither explicitly requires that a replacement handbook be provided whenever a detainee's handbook is lost or damaged, or that the handbook include information on how to contact community organizations, DHS Office for Civil Rights and Civil Liberties, or diplomatic or consular personnel.	NPREC—The handbook should include the Office for Civil Rights and Civil Liberties' phone number because the Office for Civil Rights and Civil Liberties' mandate focuses on investigating cases, whereas the OIG's mission focuses on ensuring the integrity of DHS functions.[b] ICE —Although no written ICE policy explicitly requires the provision of replacement handbooks to detainees, ICE does so in practice, and the handbook's introduction advises detainees that they may request a replacement as necessary. In addition, contact information for the Office for Civil Rights and Civil Liberties, community organizations, and diplomatic and consular personnel is provided to detainees through other means (e.g., postings in detainee housing areas).
Screening for risk of victimization and abusiveness—The facility makes every reasonable effort to obtain institutional and criminal records of immigration detainees in its custody prior to screening for risk of victimization and abusiveness. Screening of immigration detainees is conducted by employees who are culturally competent.	Both include provisions related to obtaining detainee criminal histories. As discussed above, training requirements do not include the NPREC-recommended topics related to cultural competence, but the 2011 PBNDS require that employee training address "cultural and language issues."	NPREC—Reiterated the importance of providing training to facility staff to ensure that they are culturally competent. ICE—As discussed above, many state and local jails do not have the resources to provide this specialized training, but ICE could explore assisting facilities with this type of training in the future, depending on resources.
Use of screening information—Any facility that houses both inmates and immigration detainees houses all immigration detainees separately from other inmates in the facility and provides heightened protection for immigration detainees who are identified as particularly vulnerable to sexual abuse by other detainees through the screening process. To the extent possible, immigration detainees have full access to programs, education, and work opportunities.	Both require that facilities provide heightened protection for detainees who are identified as particularly vulnerable to sexual abuse, and that facilities allow detainees who are identified as particularly vulnerable to sexual abuse to have the least restrictive housing possible. Neither requires that facilities house all immigration detainees separately from other inmates in the facility.	NPREC—Reiterated that housing detainees separately from other inmates is of paramount importance because comingling denies detainees their civil status and subjects them to rules that are appropriate for convicted criminals but not for civil detainees. ICE—ICE works to ensure the safety of detainees by housing them separately from detainees and inmates of higher threat levels. It is infeasible for state and local facilities to house detainees separately by classification level and apart from inmates because of resource constraints. ICE is working to consolidate the detainee population into fewer facilities that house solely ICE detainees, which reduces the frequency with which detainees are housed together with inmates.

NPREC recommended standard	2011 PBNDS and DHS NPRM	Related comments by former NPREC Commissioners and U.S. Immigration and Customs Enforcement (ICE) officials[a]
Inmate (detainee) reporting—The agency provides immigration detainees with access to telephones with free, preprogrammed numbers to the DHS Office for Civil Rights and Civil Liberties and the DHS OIG. In addition, the agency must provide immigration detainees with a list of phone numbers for diplomatic or consular personnel from their countries of citizenship and access to telephones to contact such personnel.	Both require facilities to provide information on how to contact the DHS OIG and consular officials. In addition, the 2011 PBNDS require that facilities provide detainees with free telephone access to these parties. Neither requires facilities to provide detainees with free telephone access to the Office for Civil Rights and Civil Liberties.	NPREC—Detainee access to the Office for Civil Rights and Civil Liberties is important because the Office for Civil Rights and Civil Liberties' mandate focuses on investigating cases, whereas the OIG's mission focuses on ensuring the integrity of DHS functions. ICE—The Office for Civil Rights and Civil Liberties has indicated that it may not have the capacity to support the increased call volume that would result from free access to its number, given its limited staffing resources.
Inmate (detainee) access to outside confidential support services—All immigration detainees have access to outside victim advocates who have experience working with immigration detainees or immigrant victims of crime for emotional support services related to sexual abuse. The facility provides such access by giving immigration detainees the current mailing addresses and telephone numbers, including toll-free hotline numbers, of local, state, and national organizations that provide these services and enabling reasonable communication between immigration detainees and these organizations. The facility ensures that communications with such advocates is private, confidential, and privileged to the extent allowable by federal, state, and local law. The facility informs immigration detainees, prior to giving them access, of the extent to which such communications will be private, confidential, and privileged.	The NPRM requires that facilities provide detainees with access to support services and enable reasonable communication between detainees and service providers, in as confidential a manner as possible. The 2011 PBNDS require facilities to provide detainees with access to outside services by giving detainees the names of local organizations that can assist detainee victims. Neither requires that victims be informed of the extent to which their communications with the service providers will be private, confidential, and privileged.	NPREC—It is critical that detainees have the option to report abuse confidentially, and ICE cannot assume that detainees will know which of their communications are confidential; ICE must apprise them of this. ICE—Reiterated that the NPRM contains language requiring that facilities enable reasonable communication between detainees and support organizations in as confidential a manner as possible, but did not comment on informing victims of the confidentiality of their communications or that the communications are confidential to the extent allowable by law versus as confidential as possible.

NPREC recommended standard	2011 PBNDS and DHS NPRM	Related comments by former NPREC Commissioners and U.S. Immigration and Customs Enforcement (ICE) officials[a]
Protection of detainee victims and witnesses—ICE never removes from the country or transfers to another facility immigration detainees who report sexual abuse before the investigation of that abuse is completed, except at the detainee victim's request. ICE considers releasing detainees who are victims of, or witnesses to, abuse; and monitoring them in the community to protect them from retaliation or further abuse during the course of the investigation.	Neither includes these requirements.	NPREC—Permitting the transfer of detainees enables retaliation against detainees who report abuse, interrupts investigation processes, and makes cases less likely to come to fruition. The threat of removal or transfer is very powerful. ICE—It is not appropriate to include these requirements in the PBNDS 2011 because detention standards apply only to detention facilities; however, it is ICE, not the detention facilities, that holds the authority to transfer and remove detainees. However, ICE Directive 11062.1—*Sexual Abuse and Assault Prevention and Intervention*—directs the ICE Office of Professional Responsibility to coordinate with appropriate entities to facilitate necessary immigration processes that ensure availability of victims, witnesses, and perpetrators for investigative interviews and administrative or criminal procedures. It also directs field office directors to consider potential alternative custodial options (such as release) for detainee victims.
Data collection—The facility collects additional data whenever an immigration detainee is the victim or perpetrator of an incident of sexual abuse in custody. The additional incident-based data collected indicate whether the victim or perpetrator was an immigration detainee, his or her status at the initiation of the investigation, and his or her status at the conclusion of the investigation.	Both require facilities to maintain records when a sexual assault occurs that identify the perpetrator, among other things. The 2011 PBNDS also require that the records identify the victim. Neither specifically requires that the records identify whether the perpetrator was an immigration detainee, his or her status at the initiation of the investigation, and his or her status at the conclusion of the investigation.	NPREC—DHS should consider developing a more robust framework for collecting, analyzing, and using these data similar to the surveys performed by the Department of Justice Bureau of Justice Statistics. It is crucial for effective record keeping and appropriate administrative response to incidents that the status of the perpetrator be designated (e.g., staff, visitor, immigration detainee). ICE—The information suggested in the NPREC recommendation is generally expected to be contained in investigative files based on the requirements in the 2011 PBNDS.

NPREC recommended standard	2011 PBNDS and DHS NPRM	Related comments by former NPREC Commissioners and U.S. Immigration and Customs Enforcement (ICE) officials[a]
Recommended standards for family facilities—These consist of four standards that address screening of immigration detainees, reporting of sexual abuse, investigations, and access to medical and mental health care in family facilities. For example, they recommend that family facilities develop screening criteria to identify those families and family members who may be at risk of being sexually victimized that will not lead to the separation of families; that parents are questioned confidentially by investigators about any incident of sexual abuse, away from their children; and that all family members are offered mental health counseling when one family member is a victim of sexual abuse in the facility.	The 2007 Family Residential Standards govern ICE family facilities. Both these standards and the NPRM require the use of screening criteria for identifying those likely to be sexual aggressors or sexual victims and that facilities offer victims of sexual abuse mental health care. Neither identifies as a priority ensuring that their application does not lead to the separation of families. In addition neither specifies that facilities offer family members of victims of sexual abuse mental health care.	NPREC—Reiterated the importance of including all four of the standards the commission recommended for family facilities. Sexual victimization of a family member in a detention facility involves shared trauma, as family members must cope with the consequences. Treatment should be made available to all family members directly affected by the victimization. Family separation can be destructive and very costly. It can also increase detainees' vulnerability to sexual victimization. ICE—These standards have been implemented in practice at ICE's residential facility. For example, all residents at family facilities have access to mental health care at any time, so all facility members could receive counseling if one member is a victim of sexual abuse. The purpose of the family facility is to retain family unity, and the purpose of the screening process is to remove any detainees that would not be appropriately housed at a family facility, such as sexual abuse perpetrators.

Source: GAO analysis of DHS and NPREC documents and testimony.

Notes: NPREC also recommended that all immigration detainees be counseled about the immigration consequences of a positive Human Immunodeficiency Virus (HIV) test at the time they are offered HIV testing. NPREC explained that at the time it drafted the recommended standards, immigrants seeking legal status in the United States who were known to be HIV-positive had to seek a waiver from the U.S. Department of Health and Human Services to do so, as all people with communicable diseases of public health significance were required to do. Because of the potential consequences of a positive test for an immigration detainee, NPREC opined that it was important that detainees make an informed decision about whether to be tested or not. In 2010, the U.S. Department of Health and Human Services published a final rule removing HIV from the list of communicable diseases of public health significance for purposes of removability and inadmissibility (see 42 C.F.R. pt. 34). As a result, this recommended standard is no longer relevant.

[a]The views presented in this column are based on interview testimony provided by seven of eight former NPREC commissioners. The other commissioner was not available for comment. We refer to the former NPREC commissioners we interviewed as NPREC for the purpose of brevity in this column, but the former commissioners noted that NPREC no longer exists and that they were not speaking on behalf of the commission.

[b]The Office for Civil Rights and Civil Liberties' mission is to support DHS's mission to secure the nation while preserving individual liberty, fairness, and equality under the law. The Office for Civil Rights and Civil Liberties works to integrate civil rights and civil liberties into all of DHS's activities by, among other things, investigating and resolving civil rights and civil liberties complaints filed by the public regarding department policies or activities, or actions taken by department personnel. The OIG's mission is to conduct independent and objective inspections, audits, and investigations to provide oversight and promote excellence, integrity, and accountability in DHS programs and operations.

National advocacy organizations we spoke with generally agreed in comments they submitted on DHS's PREA notice of proposed rulemaking that the notice of proposed rulemaking includes components that could strengthen SAAPI provisions in DHS's detention facilities, but identified aspects of the proposed rule that they view as weaknesses. For example, three of the four national advocacy organizations we spoke with agreed that the standards included in DHS's notice of proposed rulemaking, if fully implemented, would significantly increase the safety of DHS detainees, but that the standards could benefit from inclusion of additional requirements, such as that forensic medical exams be provided by a Sexual Assault Forensic Examiner (SAFE) or a Sexual Assault Nurse Examiner (SANE).[3] These organizations also raised concern that DHS's notice of proposed rulemaking would not ensure timely implementation of the standards included in the rule. As DHS's PREA rule is in proposed form and subject to change based on public comments received by the department, it is too early to assess the extent to which the final rule may address these issues.

---

[3]SAFEs are health care providers (e.g., physicians, physician assistants, nurses, nurse practitioners, or midwifes) who are specially educated and clinically prepared to perform sexual assault medical forensic exams. SANEs are registered nurses and advanced practice nurses who receive specialized education and fulfill clinical requirements to perform sexual assault medical forensic exams.

Appendix VI: DHS PREA Notice of Proposed Rulemaking Compared with DOJ PREA Rule

DHS's PREA notice of proposed rulemaking adopts the overall structure of DOJ's PREA rule and exact language from various DOJ standards; however, there are certain differences between the rules' standards, examples of which are presented in table 13.

Table 13: Selected Differences between Department of Homeland Security (DHS) Notice of Proposed Rulemaking (NPRM) for Implementing the Prison Rape Elimination Act of 2003 (PREA) Rule and Department of Justice (DOJ) Final PREA Rule

Category	DHS NPRM	DOJ final rule
Definition of "sexual abuse"	Includes attempted abuse committed by detainees and staff	Includes attempted abuse committed by staff but not by inmates
Prevention planning: cross-gender viewing and searches	Prohibits cross-gender pat-down searches of female detainees absent exigent circumstances and prohibits such searches of male detainees unless, after reasonable diligence, staff of the same gender are not available at the time the pat-down search is required or in exigent circumstances	Prohibits cross-gender pat-down searches of female inmates, absent exigent circumstances, and does not address such searches of male inmates; phases in this requirement over 3 to 5 years, depending on the rated capacity of the facility
Responsive planning: forensic medical examinations	Requires forensic medical examinations to be performed by qualified health care personnel, but does not specify that they be by Sexual Assault Forensic Examiners (SAFE) or Sexual Assault Nurse Examiners (SANE)	Requires forensic medical examinations to be performed by SAFEs or SANEs where possible, and if SAFEs or SANEs cannot be made available, by other qualified medical practitioners; efforts to provide SAFEs or SANEs are to be documented
Training and education: staff training	Differs from DOJ rule on substance of training on sexual abuse, and includes definitions and examples of prohibited and illegal sexual behavior; recognition of situations where sexual abuse may occur; recognition of physical, behavioral, and emotional signs of sexual abuse, and methods of preventing and responding to such occurrences; and how to avoid inappropriate relationships with detainees	Differs from DHS NPRM on substance of training on sexual abuse, and includes the dynamics of sexual abuse and sexual harassment in confinement, the common reaction of sexual abuse and sexual harassment victims, how to detect and respond to signs of threatened and actual sexual abuse, and how to avoid inappropriate relationships with inmates

Source: GAO analysis of DHS NPRM and DOJ final rule for implementing PREA.

Appendix VII: Enforcement and Removal Operations 2008 and 2011 Sexual Abuse and Assault Provisions Inspection Checklists

ICE ERO inspected facilities according to two sets of detention standards—the 2008 PBNDS and the 2011 PBNDS—that include SAAPI provisions in fiscal years 2010 through 2013. ERO developed inspection checklist worksheets for each of these sets of standards that it uses to assess compliance during its annual inspections of immigration detention facilities. Table 14 compares the 2008 and 2011 PBNDS SAAPI standard inspection checklists.

Table 14: U.S. Immigration and Customs Enforcement (ICE) Enforcement and Removal Operations (ERO) 2008 and 2011 Sexual Abuse and Assault Prevention and Intervention (SAAPI) Inspection Checklists

2008 SAAPI provision components	2011 SAAPI provision components
PRIORITY: The facility has a SAAPI program that includes, at a minimum, • measures to prevent sexual abuse and sexual assault; • policy and procedures for required chain-of-command reporting to the highest facility official and the ICE field office director; • measures for prompt and effective intervention to address the safety and treatment needs of detainee victims if an assault occurs; and • investigation of incidents of sexual assault, and discipline of assailants.[a]	**PRIORITY:** Each facility has written policy and procedures for a SAAPI program that includes, at a minimum, • a zero-tolerance policy for all forms of sexual abuse or assault; • measures taken to prevent sexual abuse or assault, including the designation of specific staff members responsible for staff training and detainee education regarding issues pertaining to sexual assault; • procedures for immediate reporting of any allegation of sexual abuse or assault through the facility's chain-of-command procedure, and to ERO, including written documentation requirements; • procedures for detainees to report allegations;
For service processing centers and contract detention facilities, the written policy and procedure has been approved by the field office director	• measures taken for prompt and effective intervention to address the safety and medical/mental health treatment needs of detainee victims, and to preserve and collect evidence;
Tracking statistics and reports are readily available for review by the inspectors.	• procedures for referral of incidents to appropriate investigative agencies (including law enforcement agencies and ICE Office of Professional Responsibility), and coordination with such entities; • disciplinary sanctions for staff, up to and including termination, when staff have violated agency sexual abuse policies, and data collection and reporting.
PRIORITY: All staff are trained, during orientation and in annual refresher training, in the prevention and intervention areas required by the detention standard.[b]	**PRIORITY:** Training on the facility's SAAPI program is included in initial and annual refresher training for employees, volunteers, and contract personnel, and addresses all training topics required by the detention standard. The facility maintains written documentation verifying employee, volunteer, and contractor training.
PRIORITY: Detainees are informed about the program in facility orientation and the *Detainee Handbook* (or equivalent).	**PRIORITY:** Detainees are informed about the facility's SAAPI program and zero-tolerance policy for sexual abuse and assault through the orientation program and the *Detainee Handbook*. Detainee notification, orientation, and instruction must be in a language or manner that the detainee understands
	Detainees are provided the option to report any incident of sexual abuse or assault to any staff member, including a designated staff member other than an immediate point-of-contact line officer (e.g., the program coordinator or a mental health specialist)

2008 SAAPI provision components	2011 SAAPI provision components
The Sexual Assault Awareness Notice is posted on all housing unit bulletin boards.[c]	The Sexual Assault Awareness Notice, along with the names of the program coordinator and local organizations that can assist detainees who have been victims of sexual assault, is posted on all housing unit bulletin boards. The "Sexual Assault Awareness Information" brochure is distributed to detainees.[d]
For service processing centers and contract detention facilities, the Sexual Assault Awareness Information brochure is available for detainees.	
PRIORITY: Detainees are screened upon arrival for high-risk sexual assaultive and sexual victimization potential and housed and counseled accordingly.	PRIORITY: Detainees are screened upon arrival at the facility for potential vulnerabilities to sexually aggressive behavior or tendencies to act out with sexually aggressive behavior.
Detainees who are likely to become victims will be placed in the least restrictive housing that is available and appropriate.	Detainees identified as being at risk for sexual victimization are monitored and counseled, and placed in the least restrictive housing that is available and appropriate.
	The facility administrator maintains or attempts to enter into memorandums of understanding or other agreements with community service providers or, if local providers are not available, with national organizations that provide legal advocacy and confidential emotional support services for immigrant victims of crime.
PRIORITY: When there is an alleged or proven sexual assault, the required notifications to ICE, facility management, and the appropriate law enforcement agency are promptly made.	PRIORITY: Staff members who become aware of an alleged assault immediately follow the reporting requirements set forth in the written policies and procedures.
	When a detainee is alleged to be the perpetrator, the facility administrator ensures that the incident is promptly referred to the appropriate law enforcement agency having jurisdiction for investigation, and reported to the ERO field office director.
	When an employee, contractor, or volunteer is alleged to be the perpetrator, the facility administrator ensures that the incident is promptly referred to the appropriate law enforcement agency having jurisdiction for investigation, and reported to the ERO field office director. The local government entity or contractor that owns or operates the facility is also notified.
PRIORITY: There is prompt and effective intervention when any detainee is sexually abused or assaulted, and there are policy and procedures for required chain-of-command reporting.	A detainee who is subjected to sexual abuse or assault is not returned to general population until proper reclassification, taking into consideration any increased vulnerability of the detainee as a result of the sexual abuse or assault, is completed.
	PRIORITY: Any detainee who alleges that he/she has been sexually assaulted is offered immediate protection from the assailant and referred for a medical examination or clinical assessment for potential negative symptoms.
	The facility uses a coordinated, multidisciplinary team approach to responding to sexual abuse, which includes a medical practitioner, a mental health practitioner, a security staff member, and an investigator from the assigned investigative entity, as well as representatives from outside entities that provide relevant services and expertise.
	Care is taken to place a victimized detainee in a supportive environment that represents the least restrictive housing option possble (e.g., protective custody), but victims are not held for longer than 5 days in any type of administrative segregation except in highly unusual circumstances or at the request of the detainee.

2008 SAAPI provision components	2011 SAAPI provision components
	PRIORITY: Staff suspected of perpetrating sexual abuse or assault are removed from all duties requiring detainee contact pending the outcome of an investigation.
When there is an alleged sexual assault, staff conduct a thorough investigation, gather and maintain evidence, and make referrals to appropriate law enforcement agencies for possible prosecution.	The facility ensures that all investigations into alleged sexual assault are prompt, thorough, objective, fair, and conducted by qualified investigators. Written procedures establish the coordination and sequencing of administrative and criminal investigations to ensure that the latter is not compromised by the former, including the process for conducting internal administrative investigations only after consultation with the assigned criminal investigative entity or after a criminal investigation has concluded.
	When possible and feasible, appropriate staff preserve the crime scene, and safeguard information and evidence in coordination with the referral agency and consistent with established evidence-gathering and evidence-processing procedures.
Victims of sexual abuse or assault are referred to specialized community resources for treatment and gathering of evidence.	At no cost to the detainee, the facility administrator arranges for the victim to undergo a forensic medical examination by external independent and qualified health care personnel. The results of the physical examination and all collected physical evidence are provided to the investigative entity.
	Victims are provided emergency medical and mental health services and ongoing care as appropriate, including testing for sexually transmitted diseases and infections, prophylactic treatment, emergency contraception, follow-up examinations for sexually transmitted diseases, and referrals for counseling (including crisis intervention counseling).
All records associated with claims of sexual abuse or assault are maintained, and such incidents are specifically logged and tracked by a designated staff coordinator.	**PRIORITY:** The facility administrator has designated a SAAPI program coordinator for the facility
	Information concerning the identity of a detainee victim reporting sexual assault, and the facts of the report itself, is limited to those who have a need to know in order to make decisions concerning the detainee victim's welfare, and for law enforcement/investigative purposes.
	The program coordinator reviews the results of every investigation of sexual abuse or assault to assess and improve prevention and response efforts.
	The program coordinator conducts an annual review of aggregate data regarding sexual abuse or assault incidents at the facility, and presents the findings to the ERO field office director and ICE ERO headquarters for use in determining whether changes are needed to existing policies and practices to further the goal of eliminating sexual abuse.
	All case records associated with claims of sexual abuse are maintained in a secure location, consistent with the confidentiality requirements of the detention standards on "Medical Care" and "Detention Files."

Source: GAO analysis of ICE documents.

[a]According to ODPP officials, in March 2013 an ICE working group—composed of representatives from ERO, ODPP, and the Office for Civil Rights and Civil Liberties, among others—determined

priority provisions within the 2008 and 2011 PBNDS. ICE considers these priority provisions to be of most critical importance within each detention standard based on significance to issues such as health and life safety, facility security, detainee rights, and quality of life in detention.

[b]The SAAPI provisions in the 2008 Performance-Based National Detention Standards stipulate that training for employees, volunteers, and contract personnel should include recognition of situations where sexual abuse or assault may occur, and how to report knowledge or suspicion of sexual abuse or assault, among other things.

[c]The Sexual Assault Awareness Notice contains contact information for reporting sexual abuse and assault to a facility staff member, ICE officials, ICE's Community and Detainee Helpline, and ICE's Joint Intake Center.

[d]ICE's Sexual Assault Awareness Information brochure contains information on sexual abuse and assault definitions, avoiding sexual assault, and what to do if assaulted, among other things.

Appendix VIII: Comments from the Department of Homeland Security

U.S. Department of Homeland Security
Washington, DC 20528

Homeland Security

November 4, 2013

Rebecca Gambler
Director, Homeland Security and Justice Issues
U.S. Government Accountability Office
441 G Street, NW
Washington, DC 20548

Re: Draft Report GAO-14-38, "IMMIGRATION DETENTION: Additional Actions Could Strengthen DHS Efforts to Address Sexual Abuse"

Dear Ms. Gambler:

Thank you for the opportunity to review and comment on this draft report. The U.S. Department of Homeland Security (DHS) appreciates the U.S. Government Accountability Office's (GAO's) work in planning and conducting its review and issuing this report.

DHS is fully committed to protecting detainees from all forms of sexual abuse and has taken significant steps to enhance efforts in preventing, detecting, and responding to sexual abuse in its facilities. Sexual abuse should never be a consequence of detention, and the Department is committed to a zero-tolerance policy, the full implementation of Prison Rape Elimination Act (PREA) standards, and robust oversight of its facilities to ensure comprehensive implementation. DHS is proud of its recent efforts to address the issue of sexual abuse and assault in detention and will use the recommendations from GAO to further improve its work in this area.

GAO's review of U.S. Immigrations and Customs Enforcement (ICE) allegation data disclosed 215 sexual abuse allegations between October 2009 and March 2013, 15 of which were found to be substantiated. During this period of time ICE had more than 1.2 million admissions to its detention and facilities. The Department recognizes that every substantiated case of sexual abuse is significant and represents victimization that should have been prevented. Significant measures that ICE has taken toward fulfilling the zero-tolerance policy include considerable improvements to standards, training, and policies and procedures, such as:

- Strengthening of safeguards against sexual abuse and assault of detainees in ICE detention standards.
    - In the 2011 Performance Based National Detention Standards (PBNDS), ICE further reinforced the protection, reporting, investigative, and victim care requirements previously established in the 2008 PBNDS by, for example, enhancing staff training requirements, procedures for ensuring the appropriate housing of victims, protocols for conducting prompt and thorough investigations

in coordination with criminal law enforcement entities, and requirements for
individualized and aggregate review of information relating to facility sexual
abuse and assault incidents.

o PBNDS 2011 has now been implemented at facilities housing over 50 percent of
ICE's average daily detainee population (including all but one dedicated facility),
and ICE continues on an ongoing basis to negotiate its implementation at
additional facilities, with priority given to those housing the largest populations of
detainees.

o ICE has also requested a much broader range of facilities to implement the Sexual
Abuse and Assault Prevention and Intervention (SAAPI) standard of PBNDS
2011, including smaller facilities operating under the National Detention
Standards. Excluding those detainees who are held in Department of Justice-
contracted facilities, and are therefore covered by the Department of Justice
PREA rule, approximately 85 percent of ICE detainees are currently housed in
facilities that have adopted the stronger sexual abuse and assault safeguards found
in PBNDS 2011, and a total of 94 percent of ICE detainees are covered by the
safeguards in either PBNDS 2011, PBNDS 2008, or Family Residential
Standards.

• Development of an Agency-wide Directive on Sexual Abuse and Assault Prevention
and Intervention in May 2012.

o The Directive both complements and enhances the requirements established by
detention standards by delineating ICE-wide policy and comprehensive
procedures and corresponding duties of employees for reporting, responding to,
investigating, and monitoring incidents of sexual abuse.

o The Directive requires ICE personnel to ensure that the substantive response
requirements of the 2011 PBNDS are met, and that incidents receive timely and
coordinated agency follow-up.

• Clear communication of ICE's prohibition against retaliation for reporting sexual
abuse, through the development and posting of new detainee awareness and education
materials in all detention facilities.

• Establishment and nationwide deployment of a Community and Detainee Helpline
that serves as an alternative method for detainees to report sexual abuse directly to
ICE.

• Hiring of a full-time, Agency-wide Prevention of Sexual Assault (PSA) Coordinator
to oversee efforts to improve prevention and response practices, and the designation
of 62 ICE/Enforcement and Removal Operations (ERO) Field Office PSA
Coordinators to help ensure compliance with ICE sexual assault policies in each of
the agency's Areas of Responsibility (AORs)

• Development and implementation of new comprehensive training for all ICE
employees having potential contact with detainees, on their duties and responsibilities
with respect to sexual abuse and assault prevention and intervention.

2

- Establishment of a regular intra-agency working group on issues pertaining to sexual abuse in detention.

The draft report contained five recommendations with which the Department concurs. Specifically, GAO recommended that the Director of ICE:

Recommendation 1: Develop and implement additional internal controls to ensure ERO field offices' reporting of allegations of sexual abuse and assault to the Joint Intake Center (JIC).

Response: Concur. The Director of ICE acknowledges the need for thorough review and controls of allegation reporting to ICE's JIC. It should be noted, however, that all but one of the unreported allegations cited by GAO in this report occurred prior to ICE's issuance of its Directive on SAAPI in May 2012, which outlined the specific duty of each Field Office to immediately notify the JIC of any allegations of sexual abuse. Since issuance of this Directive, ICE has developed comprehensive training materials and accompanying guidance for all ICE employees who may have contact with detainees on their duties under ICE sexual abuse policies, including those related to notification and reporting. These steps have largely addressed the issue discussed in this recommendation, as indicated by the fact that only 1 of the 10 allegations cited post-issuance of the Directive was unreported.[1]

Further, ICE's Office of Professional Responsibility (OPR) does currently have some internal controls in place to review and assess ERO field office reporting of allegations to the JIC. OPR's Office of Detention Oversight routinely conducts a query search of OPR's case management system to determine the number and type of allegations filed prior to conducting facility inspections. The Office of Detention Oversight also reviews facility sexual abuse and assault files during the course of the inspection, compares those findings with the case management records, and brings to facility management and local ERO field office personnel's attention any reporting discrepancies found.

The Director of ICE recognizes the need to enhance internal controls regarding reporting, however, and is committed to taking further steps to improve in this area. In April 2013, ICE released a mandatory training course in the prevention of sexual assault and abuse for all ICE employees who may come in contact with individuals in ICE custody. The annual training provides an overview of PREA and covers ICE's zero-tolerance policy, definitions and examples of prohibited behavior, red flags and prevention, prohibition on retaliation against those who report abuse, reporting of incidents, the investigative process, and follow-up procedural requirements. ICE will augment that training by issuing supplemental guidance to ERO Field Offices reiterating the requirement to report all allegations of sexual abuse or assault to the JIC under ICE policy.

As an additional oversight measure, the ICE PSA Coordinator's quarterly report to Agency leadership, which compiles information received about all allegations or incidents of sexual abuse or assault of individuals in ICE custody, will now include any identified cases where ERO

---

[1] Although GAO reported that three of these ten allegations were unreported, two of the three had in fact been reported by ICE ERO Field Office personnel to ICE headquarters.

3

field personnel were aware of an allegation of abuse or assault but failed to report it to the JIC. Estimated Completion Date (ECD): April 30, 2014.

Recommendation 2: Clarify guidance for ICE and facility administrators on how to correctly document investigations into sexual abuse and assault allegations.

Response: Concur. The Director of ICE fully agrees that the completeness of information contained in facility files is important because it allows ICE to review how the facility responded to abuse allegations and can be a tool for facility personnel to determine how the facility could improve future prevention and response efforts. However, for contextual purposes it is important to note that GAO's review of facility files for allegations at the 10 facilities the audit team visited includes cases that originated in Fiscal Years 2010–2012. As mentioned previously, ICE has made significant strides since this time in expanding the number of detention facilities that have adopted the sexual abuse and assault standard under PBNDS 2011, PBNDS 2008, or the Family Residential Standards, all of which articulate the requirement for facilities to maintain investigative files for sexual abuse allegations that include incident information, investigative reports, and relevant medical reports and other key information. The substantial expansion of the PBNDS safeguards largely occurred after the dates of the cases reviewed by GAO.

To further reinforce ICE's expectations regarding file documentation, ICE ERO will also issue to all field offices a broadcast message that provides detailed guidance on the documentation that facility administrators are required to maintain in their general files and administrative investigative files on all cases associated with allegations of sexual assault or abuse. The guidance will be in accordance with the *Expected Practices* of Section (V)(L) of Standard 2.11 2011 PBNDS. Each Field Office Director (FOD) will disseminate and post the guidance to all facilities within the AOR, including those that are governed by the NDS. The guidance will supplement the existing requirements in the ICE SAAPI Directive, which already directs FODs to review the written policy and procedures for the SAAPI Program for all detention facilities in their AOR. ECD: April 30, 2014.

Recommendation 3: Document and maintain reliable information on the detention standards cited in facilities' contracts and agreements, and record any agreements by facilities to undergo inspection under more rigorous standards.

Response: Concur. The Director of ICE recognizes the importance of ensuring thorough record keeping and will endeavor to improve the reliability of standards cited in facility contracts. It is important to note, however, that the deficiencies in record keeping identified by GAO did not negatively impact ICE's efforts to safeguard detainees from sexual abuse or assault victimization. In all cases, the discrepancies that GAO discovered resulted in facilities being inspected against a more rigorous set of standards than those included in facility contracts. This reflects a purposeful and intentional path by ICE to encourage facilities to move to upgraded ICE standards, when possible and practicable.

However, to facilitate the ease of ICE components being able to readily identify the standards that contractually govern a facility versus upgraded standards that a facility has voluntarily agreed to adopt for inspection purposes, ERO is in the process of modifying its Facility

4

Performance Management System (FPMS) to report data on both categories of standards. The FPMS facility list, which is generated by ERO on a weekly basis, is disseminated to the ICE Office of Acquisition Management (OAQ), the Office of Detention Oversight, and other agency components. On a quarterly basis, ERO and OAQ will jointly review the ICE authorized facilities list to ensure information on both categories is accurate and up-to-date. ECD: April 30, 2014.

Recommendation 4: Develop a process to monitor the results of ERO annual inspections conducted under the 2008 SAAPI standard to ensure consistency across the inspections and completeness in how the inspections are performed, and address any inconsistencies.

Response: Concur. The Director of ICE will make every effort to ensure a uniform inspections protocol is used and will clearly convey to ICE contract facility inspectors that they are to fully review the facility's compliance with the SAAPI standard, even in the absence of an allegation. It is important to note, however, that the inconsistencies identified by GAO with regards to inspections conducted under the 2008 SAAPI standard were found only in a limited number of facilities where no sexual abuse or assault allegations had been made in the reporting period. ERO will begin meeting with the contractor on a monthly basis, beginning in November 2013, and will continually reinforce the agency's expectations with regard to the SAAPI standard as well as other systemic oversight issues. These meetings will supplement the routine telephonic and e-mail communications that regularly take place regarding specific facility concerns and inspection scheduling. ECD: April 30, 2014.

Recommendation 5: [with] the DHS Deputy Inspector General coordinate [Office of Inspector General] access to OIG hotline connectivity data

Response: Concur. The Director of ICE will immediately begin providing the DHS Deputy Inspector General with exception reporting of OIG hotline connectivity, as appropriate. Given this action, we request that this recommendation be considered resolved and closed.

Again, thank you for the opportunity to review and provide comments on this draft report. Technical comments were previously provided under separate cover. Please feel free to contact me if you have any questions. We look forward to working with you in the future.

Sincerely,

Jim H. Crumpacker
Director
Departmental GAO-OIG Liaison Office

5

Appendix IX: GAO Contact and Staff Acknowledgments

GAO Contact	Rebecca Gambler, (202) 512-8777 or gamblerr@gao.gov
Staff Acknowledgments	In addition to the contact named above, Lacinda Ayers, Assistant Director; David Alexander; Frances A. Cook; Juan Gobel; Allyson Goldstein; Eric Hauswirth; Rebecca Kuhlmann Taylor; Olivia Lopez; Alicia Loucks; Taylor Matheson; Jessica Orr; and Gloria Proa made significant contributions to this report.

GAO's Mission	The Government Accountability Office, the audit, evaluation, and investigative arm of Congress, exists to support Congress in meeting its constitutional responsibilities and to help improve the performance and accountability of the federal government for the American people. GAO examines the use of public funds; evaluates federal programs and policies; and provides analyses, recommendations, and other assistance to help Congress make informed oversight, policy, and funding decisions. GAO's commitment to good government is reflected in its core values of accountability, integrity, and reliability.
Obtaining Copies of GAO Reports and Testimony	The fastest and easiest way to obtain copies of GAO documents at no cost is through GAO's website (http://www.gao.gov). Each weekday afternoon, GAO posts on its website newly released reports, testimony, and correspondence. To have GAO e-mail you a list of newly posted products, go to http://www.gao.gov and select "E-mail Updates."
Order by Phone	The price of each GAO publication reflects GAO's actual cost of production and distribution and depends on the number of pages in the publication and whether the publication is printed in color or black and white. Pricing and ordering information is posted on GAO's website, http://www.gao.gov/ordering.htm. Place orders by calling (202) 512-6000, toll free (866) 801-7077, or TDD (202) 512-2537. Orders may be paid for using American Express, Discover Card, MasterCard, Visa, check, or money order. Call for additional information.
Connect with GAO	Connect with GAO on Facebook, Flickr, Twitter, and YouTube. Subscribe to our RSS Feeds or E-mail Updates. Listen to our Podcasts. Visit GAO on the web at www.gao.gov.
To Report Fraud, Waste, and Abuse in Federal Programs	Contact: Website: http://www.gao.gov/fraudnet/fraudnet.htm E-mail: fraudnet@gao.gov Automated answering system: (800) 424-5454 or (202) 512-7470
Congressional Relations	Katherine Siggerud, Managing Director, siggerudk@gao.gov, (202) 512-4400, U.S. Government Accountability Office, 441 G Street NW, Room 7125, Washington, DC 20548
Public Affairs	Chuck Young, Managing Director, youngc1@gao.gov, (202) 512-4800 U.S. Government Accountability Office, 441 G Street NW, Room 7149 Washington, DC 20548

Please Print on Recycled Paper.

www.ingramcontent.com/pod-product-compliance
Lightning Source LLC
Chambersburg PA
CBHW080318290526
45790CB00005B/2086